MORALITY IS FOR PERSONS

Bernard Häring

MORALITY
IS FOR
PERSONS

New York

FARRAR, STRAUS AND GIROUX

Library of Congress catalog card number: 79-154861
First printing, 1971

Parts of chapter XV were first published in the
American Journal of Jurisprudence, copyright © 1970
by Notre Dame Law School, and are reprinted by
permission of the editors. Acknowledgment is also
made to the editors of *Sign*, in whose pages
part of this book first appeared.

Published simultaneously in Canada by
Doubleday Canada Ltd., Toronto, Ontario
Printed in the United States of America
Designed by Joan Maestro

CONTENTS

v

INTRODUCTION

THE now vast literature on personalism and existentialism has been intensively studied by philosophers and theologians. There has been keen interest in the various forms and expressions of these two modern streams of thought and the ways in which they meet and diverge.

In all my writings during the past twenty-five years, I have myself followed a personalistic and existential line of thought. I have been well aware, however, of the great effort still necessary for a consistent and courageous presentation of the chief problems involved in understanding man's call to maturity, the uniqueness of each person, and the capacity to discern and reciprocate genuine love. These problems are at the very heart of theology.

The central message of the revelation in Christ, "God is Love," compels us to see everything—personal relations above all—in this light. It is my conviction that professional moralists in past decades often lost sight of this truth. We must now reexamine old and new problems in this consistent perspective.

Why do I add this book to the others in which I have tried to promote a personalistic way of thinking in an existential context? The decision was not mine alone. It came from the people who have put questions to me, who have invited me to lecture and to respond to their own problems about a personalistic understanding of the Christian message and mission. I have therefore had to clarify for myself as well as others what characterizes an existential personalism that corresponds to the present condition of the secular world and of Christianity.

One of the questions posed with new urgency to the Christian personalist is that of organization. A saving personalism cannot be served by flight to a romantic I-Thou island. We are given many choices for the organization of all humanity and must see the relationship between the most intimate communities of persons and society at large, with its ever-increasing complexity and need of cooperation. Personalism has to be expressed with greater awareness of the data of history, sociology, psychology, and anthropology. This means that we must give new formulation to the best traditions of "natural law," probably under a new name.

The title of the book, *Morality Is for Persons,* comprises a whole program for moral theology. This is a soul-searching question for us theologians: are we remaining true to our professional ethos as expressed by Christ himself, "Sabbath is made for man, not man for the Sabbath"? The whole approach to ethics, and indeed to every single moral principle, needs reexamination in each epoch; morality has to be justified by the good of persons in community and by the community of persons. Man can never be submitted to an ethics or to a moral code that would offend the dignity of the person and his sense of responsibility for the community and the future of mankind.

A great part of the material for this book was presented in lectures in a workshop at the Catholic University in Washington, D.C., in the summer of 1967. There a number of participants insisted that I should try to publish it. I am much indebted to my sister, Sister M. Lucidia Häring, M.S.C., and her secretary, Mrs. Rose DiCicco, for the patient work of transcribing the lectures from tapes. Mrs. Josephine Ryan of Springfield, Massachusetts, undertook the task of editing the text and preparing the manuscript—a task which grew when I began to rewrite, sometimes several times, whole chapters and parts of them. The book received its final shape during and after the lecture series which I gave at Marywood College and at Villanova University during the summer of 1969. I would like to express my deepest gratitude to Mrs. Ryan for her most generous and pleasant cooperation throughout the work. Many decisive suggestions for further elaboration came from her. Indeed, if the book has finally achieved acceptable form, the credit is largely hers. My thanks extend also to her friend Mrs. Alma Fortin, who so kindly helped with the manuscript work. And for a most helpful final review of the text, my grateful thanks go to Sister Espiritu, I.H.M., and Sister Michelle, I.H.M., of Marywood College, Scranton, Pennsylvania.

B. H.

Collegio Sant' Alfonso, Rome, Italy

MORALITY IS FOR PERSONS

1

EXISTENTIAL PERSONALISM, THE SPIRIT OF AN AGE

Only in freedom and with recognition of his dignity as a person can man respond with his whole being to the personal call of God and thus attain to that fullness of being in which God's image and likeness shines forth. Hence believers, more so than unbelievers, should rejoice that two powerful currents of thought today—personalism and existentialism—are focusing attention more and more on the need to guarantee respect for the dignity and freedom of each individual human being in accordance with the time and circumstances of his existence.

At all times, but especially today, man's innermost being revolts against a philosophy of utilitarianism, the concept of a managed humanity, an anonymous world, and against all tendencies that allow the "toolmaker"—whether scientist or politician—to determine the future of humanity without intelligent regard for the meaning of human existence. Personalism gives expression to this protest and concentrates on the

3

loving relationship of the I and Thou and We. Existentialism encounters personalism in its focus on the individual in the historic and societal circumstances of personal existence. It finds expression today chiefly in revolt against conformism, especially against stereotyped traditions and structures that have no meaning in the context of today's life. When such formalism and meaningless verbiage are encountered in religion, the reaction can become most intense.

We have witnessed today the emergence of a tremendously dynamic society with new knowledge, new needs, and a totally new frame of thought, in a world largely governed by structures too static to accommodate it. The present situation can be described as one of coexistence—but not a peaceful coexistence—with this dynamic society on the one hand, and outmoded structures and habits of thought, meaningless rituals, and customs left over from a completely different milieu and a narrower basis of knowledge on the other.

Because influential men and organizations have failed to encourage the flow of new possibilities into the stream of economic, social, and religious life, we are experiencing now an existential gap, with the turbulence that inevitably accompanies discontinuity. Tensions exist between the impersonal forces of regulation on the one hand and an urgent consciousness of the existential person on the other.

Some of these tensions concern moral laws formulated in another age, expressed in terms and justified by conditions prevailing in a pre-scientific epoch but inapplicable today. Other tensions exist between a mass society that tends toward uniformism in modes and expressions, and democratic recognition of the uniqueness and freedom of each individual. We are all threatened by the depersonalization of various forms of collectivism, where persons are "units" and conformism replaces individual responsibility. There are too many structures that threaten the liberty of persons and of smaller groups. And there is widespread suspicion of many of those in power: a suspicion that they are not using their authority for the development of persons or for a community of persons but in a bureaucratic way or for the sake of power itself.

From all these diverse pressures there has arisen a healthy

passion for authenticity and freedom. But this passionate desire can sometimes lead to violent protest and to destruction of existing patterns and structures before new ones can be prepared for a humane and effective kind of progress. Thus, harm can come to the human person and his development, as in the case of outdated forms of institutions and thought.

Much of today's existential thinking and acting must be understood in the light of this actual situation of rapid transition and the tensions generated by the interaction of an urgent dynamism and a too-stubborn traditionalism or institutionalism.

The final tension is between the outer and inner faces of modern man, the outward journey and the inward journey. Man looks outward and sees the marvelous works that his hands and mind have wrought, but, looking inward, he is desperately aware of his personal confusion, his inadequacy, his doubts about what his own place is in all this. Is he an autonomous creator building his own prison, or a co-creator with God building a better world for humanity? What is the meaning of his own existence?

PERSONALISM IN THE LIGHT OF CHRIST

Searching for an ever-deeper understanding of the existential meaning of "person" and of "community of persons," we turn to Jesus Christ, the one in whom we see the perfect realization of humanity. His uniqueness does not separate him from men but calls them all together and makes them find their own unique name in unity and solidarity. His oneness with the Father, in the Spirit, makes him one with all his brethren. He does not turn his eyes to the Father without opening his heart and his arms to all of mankind.

Christ is the Word of the Father, the Messenger and Message of the fullness of love for all ages. In his whole life, and particularly in the paschal mystery, he has evidenced this love and has called upon men to follow his way.

Through his Church, he still proclaims his Gospel—through the testimony of the saints, through her spiritual teachers, through the humble ones and the wise who can enlighten others with a deeper understanding of the mystery of God and man, through the community of faith celebrating the calling of its members and their response in the sacraments of faith and in their lives: through everything that is the harvest of his grace.

In him everything attains its true personalistic center, the point OMEGA.

Confronted with him and entrusting ourselves to him, we can come to the highést form of a personalistic and existentialistic understanding of our nature and vocation, our being called to uniqueness in community. Our lives are enkindled by him who is the rallying call. To the extent that we listen to him and respond to him by the wholeness of life, each of us finds personal fulfillment as a unique person, a never-to-be-repeated creation, with all our relationships to other persons, to today's society, and to the whole of creation.

In Christ we find the climax, the abiding meaning and appeal of Christian personalism. Since we see in him the *logos,* the Word, in whom God has created all things, we cannot conceive personalism as a closed system. It is openness to ever-new events in fidelity to the Lord of history and to our fellow men.

A TYPOLOGY OF PERSONALISM

What does modern man understand by personalism? Without attempting yet to present a "right" kind of personalism, we can note what is common to all forms. This common denominator represents chiefly a matter of balance between socialization and personalization, a question of how the person is related to other persons in the encounter that takes place in the various types of communities and societies of the world today. Knowing that the encounter of persons is vital, in personalism we study the effects of social structures on the dignity of man and the rights of each person.

The dignity and freedom of the person, in an era of unparalleled socialization and organization, is of overwhelming concern today. It is also a key concept in the *Constitution on the Church in the Modern World*: in Chapter 1 on "The Dignity of the Human Person," Article 12 says, "According to the almost unanimous opinion of believers and unbelievers alike, all things on earth should be related to man as their center and crown." The question follows: but what is man; what is his genuine meaning and destiny?

All sciences about man—anthropology, sociology, psychology, comparative cultures, political science—are intended to help us understand man's nature and human history. Focusing, then, on the experience and reflection of modern man, we approach one of the most urgent problems in theology today: namely, a personalistic understanding of the natural law.

We can profit from past efforts and theories about the natural law, but we must give stronger emphasis to the personalistic side. We ask questions that are pertinent to man *because* he is man: How does a person come to the fullness of his capacity to reciprocate love and to know what genuine love is? What are the rights of the person, whether white or black, healthy or unhealthy, useful or useless to the toolmaker, of whatever religion or cultural level: what are his rights as a person?

Today's personalism is not an abstract philosophy, not a product of thinkers in an ivory tower. There are philosophers who still think this way, remote from the realities of life, but they are not listened to by those who shape the future; they evoke no warm response. Only those philosophers and theologians are heard today who have themselves intently listened to the experience of men, to their problems and questions, their anxieties and hopes, and perhaps have shared these in their own sufferings and in compassion with their fellow men. Such men are listened to even though they may offer a questionable solution or a wrong slant. I think, for example, of Harvey Cox's *The Secular City*, which I believe—from the viewpoint of faith in a personal God—has a wrong slant, but throughout the book one finds the fervor of life, an expression of what really exists, a search for needed action.

We are in an epoch that demands this forthright expression

and this search for answers to realistic questions: How do we see the present situation of mankind? What is to be done now if we wish to profit by the present opportunities? What are the positive elements today? What are the dangers? What kind of thinking makes an impact on the man of today? How can we communicate with each other?

SEARCHING SELF-EXAMINATION OF THEOLOGY

One of the chief concerns and main themes of my whole theological work—which will be synthesized to some extent here—is how to overcome the severance between life and religion. This severance is the result of many things, but one of its chief causes is that over the past few centuries a static form of theological expression has lost touch with man, who, by his very nature, is dynamic.

A certain desire for safety resulted in an immobilism which discouraged attempts to keep pace with man's social and scientific development. A so-called "safe" theology, by confining itself to mechanistic repetition, avoided the burning issues, new exigencies, new language, and personal agonies faced by modern man. The result was that forms of expression that were once meaningful eventually became only formalisms, and religion lost its significance for many who had the most influence on the thinking of their times.

Not long ago I had a talk with a typical example of this old kind of formalist, an angry old man who complained that the young men in his college were not appreciative. They should be very grateful, he said, because the college offered them "only the very best philosophy and theology according to the safe formulations of Thomas Aquinas." At the moment, a survey disclosed that a higher percentage of students at this particular Catholic college, with its "very best, safe theology" and its appropriate responses to Moses Maimonides and Averroës of the twelfth and thirteenth centuries, was experiencing more notable loss of faith than were the students in the secular colleges of the same area.

This is not happening in only one college or one religious community; we can all say "through my fault." St. Peter said, "Judgment begins with the household of God," and since God's judgment begins there, our own examination of conscience has to begin there. Have we not sometimes promoted the "God is dead" theology by our own attitudes, by fossilized structures and formulas? How often have we promoted unbelief by not living our own beliefs? Is not existentialism largely atheistic because of our failure to respond to existential problems and needs with an existential thought of our own?

But it is not only in religion that existentialism rebels against barren formalism. Existentialism is a reaction ultimately against "the establishment"; that is, wherever institutions, structures, and laws have become ends in themselves, and because of this selfish goal, their existence can no longer be justified. This is why existentialism speaks in terms of "authenticity," "identity," "being one's own self." It focuses on freedom and spontaneity, on self-affirmation in freedom, and on creativity. It believes in the importance of the ever-new beginning or, as we Christians would say, of the grace of the new beginning.

SOURCES OF TODAY'S PERSONALISM

Today's personalism is vastly different from that of the Stoics or Boethius, the great philosopher of the early sixth century and "the last of the Romans." Boethius's approach was in the style of Greek and Latin thought, through abstract reasoning, beginning, however, with ideas which were related to the prevalent culture. His definition of person was *rationalis naturae individua substantia*—"a rational nature in individual substance." He conceived of man above all as a thinker and described the ideal man, the essence of man, in relation to a system of ideas. But about the flesh-and-blood man on the street, one could say with the Stoics as well as with the pagan priests, *"Odi profanum vulgus et arceo"*—"I hate this uncultivated and profane crowd of people." This kind of personalism, based on a certain amount of rationalism, was a typical expression of a restricted upper class. Theoretical thought was the mark of a perfected or cultivated person.

People today have little interest in such abstract thought. The starting point of modern personalism is the individual as a person in a concrete world. The immediate focus is on the person and his relation to other persons and to society.

The *Pastoral Constitution on the Church in the Modern World,* in response to the vital needs of our age, affirmed this view by focusing on man and his individual and societal relationships. Not all philosophies of religion have started here. Even some types of religion did not focus on the unique value of each person. Some, like Buddhism, have attempted to eliminate from man's intricate nature his passions and desires, which means not only his pride but all his vital interest in real life: to eliminate from the person all existential responsibility for the world.

In Animism, which saw all things as sentient, the plant had essentially the same value as man. Many Hinduists even now would rather allow human persons to die by starvation than touch the "holy cows." There was a time, too, when man was defined chiefly as a "political animal," as useful to and to be used for political goals. Even so, some effort was made to protect man and some of his basic rights, although these rights were often defined more in terms of political utility than in view of the uniqueness of each person.

There were also philosophies which considered nature as a whole as something already established, and man as a person had to submit to the establishment of his biological nature. There were many philosophies about the essence of man as a being, which paid no special attention to personal relationships. Even the relationship to God was represented as something additional to man's substance.

All these may somehow be meaningful if we look at them in their historical context, but the existential background of today's personalism is very different. Today, through technology, mathematics, and the natural sciences, man has achieved power over nature—he can transform it and can either subject it to the service of the person or else sacrifice the dignity of the person to economic utility. A personalistic philosophy and theology today, therefore, must express a vital concern for the uniqueness of each individual person and for the hopes and anguish of all humanity.

We must frankly recognize the novelty of the present situation. We have acquired a new awareness, a new frame of thought, a new vocabulary, and a new historical context. We cannot simply manipulate old language and old principles and turn out the solutions needed today. The problem goes much deeper than that. The present age has a whole new spirit. I would not go so far as to say that we have a different species of man—he is still the same species as during the Ice Age and pre-scientific times—but we have a new type of person. The human spirit has a new shape about it. And this changing will go on whether we like it or not.

A grandfather who does nothing but deplore all change, whose mind is rooted in the past, will never shape the future. The alert Christian, however, will observe positive values and opportunities. In the events of this new age he perceives the groaning of a created universe, the striving of man toward redemption, toward a share in the liberty of the sons and daughters of God. This liberty—and the yearning of the world to have a share in it—is one of our chief themes. In response to the spirit of our times, we will focus attention strongly on the idea that religion and life must be brought together. Religion must become the vital experience of the presence of God to men today, a message communicated and related to *this* man, in today's language and according to to-day's type of action.

In the Bible, God always spoke to individual man and to people in the concrete historic situation, according to the language and the experience of the times. He still does. Religion must always be communicated in this way. We cannot reconcile religion and life today unless we realize the meaning of a personalism that is vitally concerned with the relation of man-to-man in the context of the actual experiences, hopes, and problems of today.

I mention only one example: the greater emphasis on con-jugal love. When life was generally lived within the context of the patriarchal family, where there were no strangers and the relationships were clear-cut, the identity of the individual was felt chiefly within this larger group. Particular emphasis on the relationship between spouses was not so necessary. But in our age of the nuclear family, man feels anguished in an impersonal society where he counts only as a number, and he has greater need for the close conjugal relationship in which he is acknowledged truly and fully as a person. He refuses to choose his marriage partner simply with a view to economic situations or for social reasons. If he does, he is considered immature, since today more than ever before this is felt to involve self-destruction of the person in his capacity to re-ciprocate genuine love.

Modern man's urgent need is that there must be a place where he is taken seriously as a person and not judged only according to utilitarian or functional norms. In *The Philoso-phy of Existentialism* Gabriel Marcel describes the problem with a certain sadness:

> Travelling on the underground, I often wonder with a kind of dread what can be the inward reality of the life of this or that man employed on the railway—the man who opens the doors, for instance, or the one who punches the tickets. Surely everything both within him and outside him conspires to identify this man with his functions—meaning not only with his functions as worker, as trade-union member or as voter, but with his vital functions as well. The rather horrible expression "time table" perfectly describes his life: so many hours for each function. Sleep, too, is a function which must be discharged so that the other functions may be exercised in their turn. The same with pleasure, with relaxation; it is logical that the weekly allowance of recreation should be determined by an expert on hygiene; recreation is a psycho-organic function which must not be neglected any more than, for instance, the function of sex. . . . As for death, it be-comes, objectively and functionally, the scrapping of what has to be of use, and must be written off as total loss.

Personalism places a new emphasis on friendship. The need is especially felt in religious communities. They want to be communities of loving persons joined in friendship and with common concerns. Friendship at all levels, friendship between superiors and sisters or confreres, should be the prototype of life. Impersonal administration makes a religious community meaningless and sterile. All this has to be given expression today in a different way, with a new kind of zeal. The discussion about celibacy also has to be understood in terms of this new concept of life.

The tremendous progress of modern psychology, the social sciences, social psychology, and history enables us to be the first generation that can take a comparative view of all existing cultures and look back on past cultures in the light of these new insights. At the same time the dynamism of our society and culture does not permit us to be rooted too much in the past. We are anxious to know about past history, to contemplate what has already happened, but our main interest is with a view to understanding the present and to help us with technological and social planning for the future.

As the *Constitution on the Church in the Modern World,* Article 4, puts it: "While man extends his power in every direction he does not always succeed in subjecting it to his own welfare." I think this is one of the most pertinent remarks that can be made about the present age. Man extends his power in all directions, he is informed about so many things, but he often does not yet know what his true welfare is and has definitely not succeeded as yet in subjecting all these new powers to the welfare of persons as persons.

There are tremendous prospects and possibilities for the future. A few years ago Italian television presented a series of programs regarding the future of man in which they interviewed about thirty professors here in America. The Italian people wanted to know what Americans thought about this subject. I took part in the program while teaching at Yale Divinity School, and I felt that the occasion—a Catholic priest teaching at a Protestant seminary and participating in a program along with numerous scientists—spoke well for the future of man. That is a dynamic aspect of the present age indicative of courage, trust, and confidence in the course of the future.

THE OPPORTUNITY FOR AND THREAT TO
PERSONS

The possibilities are almost endless. Modern science has now come close to the point of being able to change the genetic constitution of man. This may be a blessing if many causes of degeneration can be eliminated. But the many new possibilities also give rise to a horrifying uncertainty about our future. Like children playing with matches, nations with stockpiles of atom bombs can start quarrels and the whole world can burn. Within hours man and his future could be annihilated.

Man has undreamed-of powers over his own nature, but is he capable of governing these powers, of giving them the right direction so that they will truly serve humanity? For these and many other reasons man needs desperately to develop a more profound critical sense. He is now, in a totally new sense, faced with the old question: What is man? What is the person and what should he be?

Through many generations, probably through hundreds of thousands of years, man lived in a very circumscribed environment—a tribal environment or a narrow milieu. There were dissensions and variations, of course, but these differences were as nothing compared with the enormous variety of cultures and subcultures with which most of us are confronted today. In a circumscribed environment, when philosophers and theologians saw only men who acted much as they themselves did, what was common to all was considered "natural." Because men acted in a certain way in Athens or in Paris or in northern Italy, this became for philosophers or theologians the very "nature of man." When we read their long treatises on natural law today, we can date and locate the individual authors without any difficulty.

In those days even thinkers were not very critical; but modern man today is highly critical. Mass communications daily bring us into contact with multiform cultures, a great variety of events, philosophies, and problems. We are flooded with all kinds of information. And in many countries there is a democratic system which allows people to decide who will legislate and govern for them, while in others new tyrants and establishments have invented terrible methods of brainwashing. This in itself promotes a critical sensitivity.

Men and women belonging to religious orders, and modern priests, too, have learned to be more critical; they no longer accept everything—customs, laws, or theories—without questioning. They have become a kind of ferment of imaginative criticism that can help the Church and the world move toward more mature discernment.

MAN COMES OF AGE

The influence of milieu on man's freedom and on the whole shape of his "nature" is now the subject of systematic study. On the other hand, there is growing recognition that man's freedom in the social sphere can influence the milieu and consequently shape and reshape his life and future.

We have a different conception today of man's reliance on divine providence. We are no less certain and grateful that God's providence supports our whole lives, but we see the operation of his providence in a different way. We see that God has given man the power to discover solutions to more and more of the problems that have beset him in his long upward climb. More and more areas are entrusted to man's own responsibility in a totally new way. Of course, there remains a great deal that man does not know, and in those matters he must rely totally on divine providence by way of humble acceptance. But for the things about which he has already gained knowledge, which give him power over his fate, he truly acknowledges the providence of his Creator by using this knowledge and power in a responsible way on all possible occasions.

Just as a loving father gives to his growing son greater freedom and responsibility as he grows in wisdom, so God has given to man more and more responsibility for shaping his own way of life. We see this increased knowledge and power at work on all levels. Think only of the transformation of agriculture through man's growing knowledge and interference with nature. When I was a boy on the farm, we were very proud if we had a cow that gave ten or twelve kilos of milk a day. Today such an animal would be sent to the stockyards. The cow is bred as a milk producer; its "nature" has changed. Likewise, as a result of modern medical techniques, the course of nature in human beings can be manipulated more and more.

So man has a wholly new sense of being the governor of his own nature. But the vital and terribly urgent question is: How wisely will man govern? What direction will he take? Will it be for his benefit or for his final self-destruction?

This is the general picture that must be kept in mind today when we speak of personalism. There are encouraging trends toward greater freedom and respect for persons but also, unfortunately, many shocking events—including those connected with such names as Hitler, Stalin, Mao Tse-tung. Men like these—dominating others, using others callously as means, depersonalizing those within their power—can be found on all levels. We are also unfortunately faced by their heirs who approve and implement their crimes.

From my own experience I can cite an example of how their utilitarian philosophy works. The Russian nurse with whom I worked when helping Russian civilians during the last war told me that her parents were "eliminated" in a concentration camp, and strangely she approved of this wholeheartedly, because those "silly people" had openly and emphatically declared that God exists! She also told me she had heard of twenty million people who were disposed of by being sent to labor camps in Siberia, where they died. This she found quite normal.

Such experiences and other recent events that could be cited have horrifying implications for the future of man. What are we to think of the education of such a person—a form of psychological manipulation resulting in a woman's wholehearted approval of the killing of her own parents and the enslavement and death of twenty million innocent people? What of the boast of Mao Tse-tung that China will not be greatly harmed by the loss of one or two hundred million people in a war with "the imperialists"? What of the calculation of the advisers of the American presidents regarding the matter of unconditional surrender, of 152,000 persons killed in one moment and 300.000 rendered unfit to live a normal life?

Calculations . . . How much will these political calculations cost the future of man? And how much will individual calculations of this kind cost? What will happen, for example, to the "nature" of mothers if abortion becomes a "normal" means of birth control?

Yet such things are being experienced today. Millions upon millions are being killed, enslaved, maimed, and driven from their homes for political reasons. There are abuses of power by manipulators in both the free and the unfree worlds. There is heartless management on the highest levels—sometimes even in the medical world—management without concern for the dignity and genuine freedom of the persons involved.

In a series of evening lectures held at Yale University in 1967 on the future of man, an economist spoke about this theme of human management on the economic level. He held that the toolmaker makes men; that the progress of natural sciences and technology by itself will determine the future of man. There were many comments by troubled professors and students after that lecture. Who determines technology? Is man to be subject to the dynamism and automatism of technology?

There is deep anguish today about man's being only a cog in the process of life. He is afraid of having only an instrumental value, and if there is only an instrumental value, he is even more afraid of having no reason for being at all.

Anguish and superficiality are the characteristic marks of the timid victims of overpowering institutions, establishments. and unhealthy public opinion. Are we not daily confronted by people who are unable to find themselves but who nevertheless yearn for a dignified personal life? Even good, intelligent people are so strongly affected by the power of public opinion that some who would prefer to respect the dignity of each human being would, with scarcely any reflection, agree to an abortion if there seemed to be danger that a child might be born deformed or otherwise socially unacceptable. In some new environments no serious discussion of the new "dogma"—that abortion is justified by any serious inconvenience to the family or society—is possible, since no one asks insistently: Is the unborn child a person or not? The personalist insists that this question relates not just to the dignity of each embryo but to the dignity of all mankind.

During Hitler's regime hundreds of thousands of retarded children and other "unfit" persons were annihilated, and this attitude prevails today among some advocates of situation ethics even in free countries. The ideal of utility dominates to such an extent that even a society built on respect for all persons tends to countenance some form of annihilation for those who, from the viewpoint of economic progress, are considered "unfit."

It is against all this that the genuine personalist must protest. His reaction is healthy and is evidence of a new sensitivity that resulted from the shock of actual experience. He asks that consideration be given not only to utility but to persons as persons: as an I to Thou, and with the Thou to We. Then the emphasis must be on genuine self-fulfillment, on the determination to think of persons not only for their functional role but as persons: for their contributions as persons and for the respect owed to them as such.

A man who has come of age is a personalist concelebrating his existence with fellow men in responsibility, freedom, and discernment. Otherwise, he has not "come of age."

2

PERSONALISTIC APPROACHES TO THEOLOGY AND NATURAL LAW

BECAUSE a person must know, above all, that he is taken seriously as a person by God, the personalistic approach to religion must be constantly emphasized. It must set the tone for theology and for all forms of life in the Church. Only thus can the Church become a personalizing reality for all mankind.

God—a personal God—calls persons to communion in fellowship as the first disciples were called together as friends around Christ.* The covenant between God and man—religion—can be seen as the prototype of I-Thou-We personalism, because God takes us seriously. Indeed, he does not need us, does not gain anything from us; but he loves us and wishes to be loved by us without any recompense besides love. And

---

* This perspective can be seen in my first book, *Das Heilige und Das Gute* (Erich Wewel Verlag, Freiburg), on the relation between religion and morals, and especially in the first two volumes of my *Law of Christ*, which focuses chiefly on religion as vocation—the encounter of persons in community.

we, on our part, are to take him seriously in his love, and not only insofar as we need him for our earthly wants or for our individual salvation, or as a "means" for anything. Religion is response in faith, joy, hope, fellowship in word and love. And thus it brings wholeness and salvation of persons.

In this perspective, morality can never involve merely an abstract, lifeless system of imperatives, an accumulation of laws or precepts. It has to do with love for love, the response of a person living in a community of men to the individual call of the living God, a response throughout the whole of life. All God's gifts, the welfare and needs of our brothers and sisters, all the opportunities of the day become a part of the calling. And grace—the gracious presence of God, the operations of the Holy Spirit, who vivifies us—is of no avail unless we respond as persons, realizing in joy and gratitude that everything we are and all we possess are gifts of God and are to be received not only for utility's sake but as a response to his expression of love.

THE VOCABULARY OF CHRISTIAN PERSONALISM

Christian personalism has its own vocabulary which expresses this characteristic outlook. When preaching, teaching, writing, or discussing, we must not "thingify" the reality of God and man and the covenant between them. There have been ascetical writings in the past without any personalistic touch about them, but they no longer move men. A true response to the anguish, joy, and hope of men today necessitates a new style sensitive to the dignity of each man in his experience as a person among persons.

The unique possibilities of each "I" can only be realized in view of the Thou and We and to the extent that I regard the possibilities of my neighbor as seriously as I regard my own. Ethics has to do with responsible love, not just any kind of "love" such as in the ethics of romanticism or sentimentalism—a mere "falling in love" and falling out of love and no more. Emphasis must be placed on maturity, discernment, spontaneity, creativity, and on the individuality of each unique person.

A similar change in emphasis must be made particularly in efforts to rethink and rewrite theological treatises on the natural law, as well as on the commandments and sacraments. For example, if one opens any of the so-called classical manuals of moral theology (by Aertnys-Damen, H. Noldin, Tanquerey, M. Zalba, etc.), one finds that they are all alike. First they deal with the ten commandments, then the thousand and one precepts of the Church—although the latter are given more serious treatment than the "law of love" and the ten commandments, especially if it is a question of the sacred property of the Church, sacred vestments, sacred rituals, and other sacred things. Then, after all this, come the sacraments, but they are presented chiefly as sacred things to be used as means to fulfill all the other precepts, and a new circle begins of innumerable precepts "under pain of mortal sin." Often there is no explanation of how these matters relate to the welfare of a person as a person in community and involved in human relationships. A classic example of this impersonal, utilitarian approach can be found in the Acts of the Roman Synod (1961), where it says, *"Fidelibus inculcandum est ut saepe utantur his sacris rebus"*—"It must be inculcated in the faithful that they have to use these sacred things frequently."

Many books about the sacraments dealt with administration rather than with the celebration and proclamation of the good news. They stressed such ideas as jurisdiction, the scrupulous enunciation of Latin words understood by nobody except the priest, the uniformity of texts, and accurate gestures: in a word, accurate "administration." Marriage was expounded chiefly as a means of reproduction and couched in juridical terms with emphasis on "validity"—the managerial style. This was the approach to theology in much of the Church before the Second Vatican Council. Thank God, a more personalistic approach and practice prevailed in other parts of the Church.

The council's perspective is marked by a personalistic understanding and language: God speaks to his people, Christ is still proclaiming the good news, the people of God respond to him (*Constitution on the Sacred Liturgy,* Article 33). We do not just use things or means; we speak about an encounter with God. We listen to the Lord, rejoice in him, and are together united in him in fellowship through the Holy Spirit —a communion of persons in the celebration of the sacraments and in a sharing of genuine love. From this point on, the whole style of living, nourished by this experience, becomes more personalistic. But theology and catechetics still have a tremendous amount of work to do before overcoming all impersonal tendencies toward magic and extreme "sacralization."

A personalistic outlook and terminology are particularly necessary in the matter of conscience. It becomes evident, for instance, that one cannot form one's conscience as a Christian personalist merely or chiefly by looking to abstract principles. A personalistic conscience is always confronted with the living God and his gifts, and with one's brother or one's enemy, who is in need of love. God's gifts—the talents he has given us— are his appeal to us. In our whole constitution and concrete experience, we are his message and his messengers for our brothers. When we understand ourselves in this light, we understand his word in whom we are created, as is our brother, our fellow man.

Nor can we ever look upon the needs of our fellow man merely as an occasion for us to observe principles or earn merits. Morals are not part of some commercial system. In Christian morality there is a place for reward, but a reward which is inherent in love. God in his infinite love, the concelebration of his love, is our reward. The other—the neighbor, the brother—is revered because we encounter Christ in him when confronted with his love or his needs. Each bears a unique name. He must be loved and revered as a person. Christ appeals to us in this situation, puts us to the test as to whether we recognize him, and by our response to our neighbor, we make a return to him for all he has given us.

In all the vital areas of moral theology, and to all the faithful, whatever the level of their sophistication, this personal thinking must be communicated. We must give much greater emphasis to smaller groups: to marriage and the family, where the fundamental experience and expression of love can be learned. And beyond marriage and family, we must try to understand better, in a personalistic way, the great testimony of celibacy—of loving persons, understood first as persons, of revering all others beyond and above sexual gratification, of serving everybody in unselfish love.

This is the power of the kingdom of God: Christ, beyond and above all the urges of this world, has one universal vocation to manifest unselfish love and the power of the love that gathers us around himself. Then human sexuality will also be approached in a thoroughly personalistic way. Personalism takes the body as well as the spirit seriously. The body can become more and more an expression, a gift, an invitation to love.

Every aspect of Church life, including canon law, must be tested by a personalistic conscience and consciousness: Does the Church herself manifest the community of disciples gathered around the Lord, living apart from the world's pride and frustration but in openness to the signs of the times, in openness to each other, with no segregation into separate classes? Christianity knows nothing of two classes, one called to perfection and another subject only to abstract, minimal precepts. There must be recognition for a variety and richness of forms of life, of roles and functions—but not barren roles and functions. The dominant value must always be the person in his capacity to reciprocate love, and thus the person in his growth toward maturity.

The Church must have its finances, administration, and chanceries, but they must be tested by conscience as to whether such structures protect and encourage the community of love or conceal it.

This reexamination extends to our secular as well as our ecclesiastical structures and establishments. Are they flexible enough to protect the liberty of man? Do they foster a true kind of liberty?

We must study the tremendous ramifications and the great power of economics to plan our lives, in order to find ways to inspire it with more respect for persons. Concern for utility is necessary, but it must be given direction by the final power of discernment and firmness which enable men to initiate and foster whatever enterprises are necessary for the service of man as a person and of a genuine community of persons. If each one of us really takes seriously his own responsibility for the general milieu, and if we unite all our efforts, the milieu can gradually be transformed for the benefit of persons in all their relationships with each other.

NATURAL-LAW FORMULATIONS WITH A VIEW TO PERSONS

All these urgent needs mean that the concept and the formulation of the natural law need to be restudied in order to clarify our understanding of the real nature of man as a person in community.

As Christian personalists and existentialists, our viewpoint must always be that of the individual man or woman in communion with the personal God of history. We have outgrown the viewpoint of an immobile order of things expressed by a natural-law philosophy chiefly concerned for the conservation of the status quo. The immobile God of Aristotle and Parmenides is not our God. Parmenides, and many other thinkers who overemphasized the static aspect of life, lived in the stability of a closed tribal society, and we can understand how for them truth was perceived in terms of unchangeable, abstract principles and ideas. Since the images of God and man are related to each other, this conservative mentality finds consolation in the thought that the absolute immobile is divine, that the perfection of God is that he never changes. Enthroned above a stable world, he calls for immobile persons and structures, and he never disturbs our circle. The other extreme is a Heraclitean passion for movement with little concern for continuity. Here God becomes just an expression of the dynamism of history or of "the open future" of the world.

In our approach to a Christian existential personalism, all these fundamental problems must be examined, as well as the implications of failing to propose any.

Since we do not have to express ourselves for the benefit of past generations, we must examine the vocabulary in use today. At least some of the questions posed in earlier manuals must be reproposed in a new style, but many other questions will not be asked any more. Problems die and new ones are born, and each generation has to face its own situation.

I hope, for instance, that a type of questioning I once heard in Rome will never be brought up again. When I first came to Rome in 1948, I attended a gathering of priests at which cases in moral theology were discussed by "very competent men." The speaker dealt with three "very important" types of cases. The first had to do with the right of privileged persons to hear mass in a private chapel reserved for cardinals or bishops. The second question was whether a priest serving mass for another was allowed to open the mass book and turn the page after communion. It was shown that this is prohibited by the Supreme Authority, which has a divine mandate, and therefore it is done probably under grave sin but at least under venial sin. The argument was serious, since several responses of the Sacred Congregation of Rites could be quoted on the matter. And the third question was whether a priest can leave the corporal unfolded if he knows that immediately after him, on the same altar, another priest will say mass. Once more there were clear responses from the Supreme Authority that all this is absolutely forbidden.

The whole discussion was carried on with utmost seriousness by the moral theologians and canonists. I had previously spent some years in Russia with the German medical corps looking after the needs of soldiers and civilians; I had personal experience of life in a prison camp and of how war refugees lived; I realized that in Italy communism was at that time an imminent danger. You can imagine my amazement!

Of course, this kind of game with nothingness never involved the greater part of the Church. But have we really overcome all such forms of estrangement? Is there enough prophetic spirit in the Church today that really sees and feels the needs of man passionately? Does our theological and spiritual talk really foster the kind of prophetic spirit that brings life and religion constantly together?

3

EXISTENTIAL OPENNESS TO NEW APPEALS AND CONTINUITY

Today's world is shaken by the tension between different forms of a kind of "security complex" and the impatient desire to embark on new, daring, and risky paths. Between being and becoming, we are experiencing the pangs of childbirth. Existentialist thinkers have tried to give expression and shape to this "spirit of the times," viewed by the security-minded with anguish and regarded by the innovators with a feeling of exultation.

The word "existentialism" comes from the Latin word *existere*, meaning "going out": having the courage of becoming, being one's self in freedom with all its risks, and with a firm resolve not to live a life of artificial isolation but to go out from individual loneliness toward the Other and toward ever-new situations and possibilities.

The existentialist, as an outgoing person, is concerned about his own identity and authenticity and has an attitude of healthy self-respect in his encounter with the Other and with all creation. Personalistic existentialism is not of itself a one-sided concern for being and becoming ever more one's own self. It can degenerate into that, to be sure, but more authentically it means becoming increasingly one's whole self, chiefly with a view to a more authentic encounter with the Other.

Crucial questions debated by today's existentialism are the evaluation of institutions, structures, and traditions, and the proper understanding of history. Existentialism can be merely a violent protest against meaningless patterns of life, a discarding of the old without concern for creating new forms of life. It can simply mean distrust of all forms of continuity, the desire to live only in the present without gratitude for the past and without responsibility for the future. It can mean a trend toward anarchy. But there are many existentialistic expressions of life and forms of thought that give even greater values to the here and now and its free expression by seeing this against the fuller background of past and future, person and community, spontaneous and unique creativity, and life going on not without, but specifically with, the help of flexible structures and institutions.

CONCRETE FORMS OF EXISTENTIALISTIC PHILOSOPHIES

Among the best-known representatives of existentialistic thought today are Jean-Paul Sartre and his friend Simone de Beauvoir. Their chief concern is always for a constantly new and ever-changing demonstration of individual freedom. They put much more emphasis on becoming than on being. They demonstrate their own concept of freedom by living together in a kind of husband-wife relationship for a while and then separating for another period to show that their life as individuals and as a couple is not institutionalized.

Sartre's thought is directed toward a complete freedom, for an ever-new creation of the free individual, for a freedom in becoming, unfettered by rules or abstract principles or by any organization or tradition which could be a threat to the person who constantly is to be created and re-created in undetermined freedom. Man is responsible only to himself in the present instant.

In many forms of existentialism which follow the pattern of Sartre's thought there is strong opposition to any assertion of absolute values and especially to an Absolute Being to whom the human person should be responsible. If man has to be responsible to an Other who has the absolute fullness of being, how can he have or seek unlimited freedom of becoming? How can he continue to create his own freedom? The courage to protest against all threats to the individual's total freedom in becoming is the most vital experience for many existentialists. Yet, since this courage does not find any assurance in daily experience, the constant insecurity makes it ever necessary to demonstrate anew to one's self and to the world that "I am free."

Albert Camus was obsessed by the existentialist's characteristic concern for freedom. The individual responsible only to himself makes his own free choice according to his own situation. But Camus, who did not find his way to faith in a personal God, saw that if man has no higher responsibility than to himself, and death is the end of all things, man will find that all choices are ultimately meaningless and life is absurd. It is my personal impression that his philosophy of absurdity is meant to be an existentialist protest against a society responsible for the destruction wrought by world wars and mass crimes, which were explosions of absurdity. In a shocking way, it is a yearning for "meaning," for a world that does manifest true love and freedom.

Heidegger's existentialist thought is characterized by a somewhat broader outlook. No final cause or absolute person is postulated, but human existence is understood as an openness, or at least as the cry for an open context of life, a reaching out toward fullness of being. The quest for final meaning and freedom is even more evident in the existentialist philosophy of Jaspers.

There are also specifically Christian forms of existentialism, closer to the biblical truth of the calling of each person to particular opportunities and possibilities of love. The person discovers his real self by finding the One who calls him and by responding to the call in full recognition of his uniqueness as a person with these particular gifts and in this particular situation.

It is clear, then, that existential thought can assume very different forms and result in widely different aberrations and loyalties in the matter of continuity. Some forms, overreacting against those who cling to lifeless patterns, go to opposite extremes of arbitrariness and total discontinuity. Others, with a tendency toward social personalism, strive for vital progress, in appreciation of past experience and wisdom. Christian existentialism has its own approach to continuity—by way of its I-Thou-We personalism and the celebration of the here and now as concelebration of hope in gratitude and gratitude in hope.

THE VIRTUES OF THE CHRISTIAN
EXISTENTIALIST

The biblical "eschatological" virtues of hope, readiness, watchfulness do not allow the believer to become immobile or self-satisfied. They entail a protest against all forms of self-complacency and the inertia of establishments. The Christian existentialist must dissociate himself from the bourgeois concept of "virtue," where self-concern and desire for security take precedence over openness and the courage to take risks in life.

In the best Christian tradition, "virtue" means character, firmness of direction with an openness toward reality, toward the needs of people and of the community. It means respect for the continuity of a life with which the faithful respond to God, as Creator and Redeemer, by their openness to him who, in his own fidelity, is ever doing new things. Thus, the "virtuous" man searches for God's intention with regard to man in his own day and guarantees to God his faithful cooperation in bringing to fulfillment that divine intention.

The approach is dynamic, in total contrast to that immobilism which sometimes calls itself "fidelity to God" or "virtue" but which gives the impression that God speaks only according to the language of past ages. A conservative philosophy according to the style of the Restoration, or an ethics of "virtue" in which security plays the dominant role, does no honor to the God of continuous creation and the Redeemer and Lord of history, who calls for a constant conversion and total openness to the signs of the times.

The prophets of the Old Testament, and especially Christ, had harsh words for immobile "traditionalism." The faithful teacher of morality is "a learner in the Kingdom of Heaven; he is like a householder who can produce from his store both the new and the old" (Matt. 13:52).

CONTINUITY IN MOVEMENT

In the Bible and in man's experience generally, we find that God has worked with man in an unbroken history of movement. Everywhere it is made evident that a basic law of life is to grow, change, adapt, develop; and since the human person is the highest form of life on earth, he is most subject to this open-ended process ("law of growth"), which may be the most important aspect of "natural law." To deny or to frustrate the working of this principle in man, by formulations suggesting that life and man can stand still, is one of the gravest offenses against the natural law as well as the prophetic tradition. In this marvelous history with God, we must live according to our true nature as he designed it, by adapting in accordance with our intelligence to historical situations, and to the real possibilities of progress which God has prepared for us.

Man's dynamism and creativity, granted by God to his image, is a mirror of God's design for mankind and for each individual person, and is an essential part of the human vocation. By responding to it, man renders thanks to his Creator and gives witness to his faith that God is the fullness of life. He is for us presence and future. He is our hope.

This perspective should shed much light on many controversial questions. For example, the discussions about birth regulation can especially benefit from this approach. Instead of focusing one-sidedly on an alleged procreative finality in the "nature" of each conjugal act as a biological norm, the focus should be on total fidelity to the *creative* task of the human person and the total creative meaning of conjugal love. A responsible decision about the extent of birth control is then seen in the light of God's creative design, of his love for each person and for humanity as a whole.

Continuity of conjugal morality can only be preserved in openness to the new needs of family and society. This may well be much more demanding than an approach based either on unchangeable "traditions" and formulas or on biological laws. Man's procreative task has always been seen by wise men and women in the light of a truly creative education. It should be seen in the total context of man's creative mission in community, fellowship, society, culture. Man is faithful if in all this he is a mirror-image of the Creator's presence in his work throughout the evolution of the world and the history of mankind.

THE FAITHFUL ONE WHO MAKES ALL THINGS NEW

The Spirit of God renews the face of the earth. He calls for fidelity through conversion and renewal. Christ is the faithful one who brings everything to its completion, inserting into man's history the tremendous dynamism of his life, word, and example. In a new way and in evident continuity with the work of the prophets, Christ calls for fidelity to the fundamental ethical values: love, mercy, justice. He accepts or rejects traditions to the extent that they express or oppose these permanent values. For example, he condemned all forms of immobilism that stood in the way of the universal brotherhood of man and thus did not honor his Father. He broke away from traditions and customs when fidelity to his mission, to the great command of love, demanded it, and he warned his disciples that they must do the same. Even his words "Follow me" suggest movement, a journey toward new horizons. Discipleship also suggests continuity: one step after another in a clear direction—namely, that of true love and justice.

Christians go forward with deep gratitude to those who have opened the way in the past but with the knowledge that our present task is to prepare the way toward the future in accordance with God's design. Throughout the ages God has sent his prophets to "prepare the way," and he still sends them. We call them "men ahead of their times," but they come in God's time. We must try to discern who are the true prophets, but having discerned them, we must listen to them. Then, according to our capabilities and particular circumstances, we adapt our thinking to what God has prepared for us, and we act, move, and follow him. Thus we follow Christ, the faithful one who makes all things new.

4

PERSONALISM IN THE LIGHT OF THE PASCHAL MYSTERY

CHRIST is the Redeemer of all persons and of the community of persons. In his life we see the freshness and fullness of personal relationships: his total "being-with" others and his desire that others—all others—be with him, and thus with each other.

The disciples, attracted to him and invited by him, leave everything in order to follow him. Men and women who are outcast as sinners and obsessed by evil spirits put all their trust in him. He excludes no one from his friendship, recognizes no barriers of caste, culture, or even of reputation. In a closed, male-centered society, he initiates conversation with the Samaritan woman at the well of Jacob, accepts the signs of love given him by a woman known as a public sinner. He eats with the despised tax-gatherers and other "bad characters"; "he does not turn away from anyone who comes to him" (John 6:37).

With him "law" never takes precedence over person. When

the pharisees object that on the Sabbath he healed the man with a withered arm, Jesus looks "with anger and sorrow at their obstinate stupidity" (Mark 3:5).

Since he has come only to serve, he does not look for privileges associated with rank. When the blind beggar Bartimaeus cries out in the crowd, "Jesus, have pity on me!", his disciples tell the man to "be quiet." But Christ teaches his friends to have a new attitude of concern. He stops and bids them, "Call him." Then they cry out to the blind man, "Take heart; stand up; he is calling you!" And when the man comes, Jesus asks, "What do you want me to do for you?" This is the language of a love that does not impose one's own idea of benefits on others but looks to the real needs of neighbor. "That I may see," the blind man answered; and when he had given him his sight, Jesus said, "Your faith has cured you" (Luke 18:35-42). So he makes evident that faith is a very personal human relationship: trust in the one who is concerned for all, and a new outlook that never overlooks the person.

FULLNESS OF BEING IN DYING FOR OTHERS

No other book reveals so much about the truth of personalism in action as the Gospels. At the heart of the Gospels is the paschal mystery, whose deepest meaning and challenge is explained to us in the Farewell Discourses and the High Priestly Prayer (John 13-17). We find a key also in the last words of Jesus. While suffering the most terrifying pains and humiliation, he shows loving concern not only for the women who weep for him, not only for his mother and his beloved disciple, but for those who have crucified him. "Father forgive them; they do not know what they are doing." And he who bears the burden of all men has, in the hour of his extreme suffering, words of trust, assurance, and friendship for the thief crucified along with him.

This was Jesus' own kind of personalism, his being-a-person, his "being-with." Only if we understand it in the paschal mystery can we fully realize what true Christian personalism is.

The paschal mystery is the oneness of the life, passion, death, resurrection, ascension, and parousia of the Lord. It is not possible theologically to treat the passion and death of the Lord separately, nor the resurrection alone; we must see everything as the one paschal mystery. This is essential because we here see Christ offering himself to the Father by embracing his brothers, by delivering himself as ransom for them. He is accepted by the Father as the one who proclaimed his name and made known his fatherly love to his brothers (see Heb. 2:12). The seal of acceptance is the glory which shines on the human nature of Christ "at the right hand of the Father." The full manifestation of his being accepted as an offering for all will be his final coming as the Lord, when the glory of all his brethren and full brotherhood will be revealed as the focal point of his life and death.

One of the great themes of the New Testament is Christ's "coming from the Father and returning to the Father." This is his existence, his "ex-istent," outgoing being manifested in the Easter mystery. In the triune life of God, Christ's whole pre-existent reality is to be the Word of the Father, the expression of the Father's love; and he gives himself wholly to the Father. It is a mutual giving in the Holy Spirit, who is the bond of unity.

CONCELEBRATION OF GOD'S LOVE IN CHRIST AND IN HIS DISCIPLES

This relationship is set forth in profound and clear thought in scholastic theology when it describes the Divine Person as *relatio subsistens*. That is, the Divine Persons are not separated entities, not isolationists. They can be thought of by us only as "being-with," life and love in action. The relationship in love and truth is the fullness of being-a-person. The Father is this person by expressing all his love, his glory, his wisdom in his Word, the Son. And the Son is the Word, gift of the Father and full response to the Father. The Holy Spirit is this stream of life and love, the unifying bond, this "being-with" of Father and Son in mutual bestowal. The Bible never speaks of relationships in God's triune life without a perspective of God's "being-with" man and his world. God reveals his inner personal life through his creative and redemptive relation to man.

The coming of Christ from the Father and the returning of his human nature to the Father show humanity's intimate sharing in the love of God and the divine intention to have mankind as sharers, concelebrants of his triune love, not out of need but out of his own superabundant love.

In Greek philosophy, the concept of love was related only to a person's need of another. Aristotle and other Greek philosophers maintained, therefore, that God is not a lover; since he is perfect, he can only be the goal of all of man's love, but he cannot love or want love. However, the Christian concept of God is not of one who is perfect without love and without desire to be loved. The chief Christian doctrine is specifically that God is love and, not out of need but out of infinite love, wishes to have concelebrants of his love. For this wonderful sharing of love he has created us and redeemed us.

Christ came for all men. "God so loved the world that He sent His only begotten Son" (John 3:16). And Jesus made clear in his Farewell Discourses that he, who always "loved His own who were in the world" (John 13:1), came to manifest in this world the full extent of his love, which is also the Father's: "The one who sees me sees the Father" (John 14:9). And he promised that the Holy Spirit would come so that the world might understand the full extent of his work and his word. His disciples too should be transformed in order that their love may manifest the Father.

Christ's human nature is glorified not only because he is the Son but ultimately because he has "emptied himself" and delivered himself totally for his brethren to the glory of the Father. From the beginning, Jesus is truly the Son, but this is not fully manifested in his body until he has surrendered himself wholly and visibly to the Father for all mankind. Then the three dimensions of the love of God and neighbor are seen in Christ's full glorification. In his human nature he is fully Son, celebrating the triune love, coming from the Father, anointed by the Spirit, identified with all his brethren, bringing home all that the Father gave him (John 6:37).

The heavenly liturgy includes this total identification of Christ with all of mankind; hence, love of God is not a separate department from love of brethren. The innermost personal relationship of Christ in his divine person becomes a visible reality in his perfect relationship with his brethren. He who is the Word of the Father and is with the Father is also with us in the humanity which he took upon himself, identifying himself with us through the same human situation marked by love, joy, suffering and death.

Christ's love is a totally self-giving one. His final goal and motivation is not selfish self-fulfillment but fulfillment arising from self-surrender. He "did not come to please himself" (Rom. 15:3); he came to glorify the Father by his all-embracing fraternal love. He consecrates himself for his brethren. "For them I have consecrated myself that they too may be consecrated in truth" (John 17:19). In him and through him, religion has become life and love of persons.

His disciples, who know him to be the source of their life and the norm of their conduct, are also consecrated for a life of service, of fulfillment in self-surrender. All this must constantly be seen in contrast to Adam, the unredeemed man, prototype of the selfish, self-fulfilling personalist.

ADAMITIC PERSONALISM

In the book of Genesis the serpent inaugurated a new kind of dialogue, really a monologue, because the voice of the serpent is the voice of man's self-seeking ego. This monologue with the serpent is a human device. You will hear it in yourself and will know it as yourself, your own urge to be independent of God, as Adam and Eve wanted to be.

The outcome of this Adamitic personalism is inevitable. Adam and Eve hide themselves from God. They are not able to face a dialogue when God comes down into Paradise to talk with them in "the cool evening." (This is a wonderful expression, "the cool evening"—the imagery of human experience when, after the day's heat, people in the Orient come out and walk and talk with each other.) But when God comes to walk and talk with Adam in Paradise, Adam, because of his erroneous personalism, hides himself and is unable to meet his God.

Moreover, the bond of love between Adam and Eve is broken by the insistence of each on "self-fulfillment" in their own relationship. In their egotism they are severed from God's intimate friendship, dispersed over the face of the earth, yet chained together as persons both yearning for each other and domineering over each other.

Under the influence of the original and true personalism willed by God from the beginning, Adam received Eve with jubilation. "This is bone of my bone!" He saw Eve as a gift from God, an answer to his heartfelt desire, and was thankful. But after the self-seeking of the two persons independent of God, all was different. "It was this woman, this miserable creature Thou hast assigned to me!" Now Adam judges his wife, wants to domineer over her. There is severance between them; they are no longer partners in salvation, although they are tied together.

In the self-giving personalism manifested by Christ the Redeemer and intended by the Creator from the very beginning, man will leave father and mother and cleave to his wife faithfully in true love. But Adam's personalism shows how, when man severs his adoring relationship with God, his relationships with his fellow men also are disturbed. This severance continues. In the fourth chapter of Genesis, Lamech, the fourth descendant of Cain, takes two wives, and he talks to his women but does not talk of love. "Listen, you women of Lamech . . . I have slain a man for a small wounding . . . Sevenfold vengence shall be taken for Cain, but for Lamech seventy times sevenfold."

So fear, exploitation, polygamy, domination, appeared where God intended love. It is not merely a question of one person having caused all that we mean by original sin. Sin increased from Adam and Eve to Lamech; it has increased in and through all of us who daily sin. Our predecessors began the process, but we too are contributing to sinfulness by our own individual sins.

There has always been a choice: a pernicious solidarity with Adam and Eve or a saving solidarity which finally has been revealed in Christ. Christ, the Rock, was already, in a hidden way, with the people of Israel. He was with the saints and humble ones of other nations, to whom the Old Testament pays tribute. And he is with us through faith, especially in the community of faith.

Through the paschal mystery, he has redeemed us from Adam's self-centered personalism and has directed us toward his own I-Thou-We personalism, wherein he gives himself wholly to the Father and to his fellow men. When we freely choose the outlook of the redeemed personalist offered us by the gracious love of Christ and the power of the Spirit, we have redemption in action.

THE PERSONALISM OF THE REDEMPTION

The letter to the Hebrews (10:5-7) reveals that Christ's sacrifice is not something apart from the fullness of his mission. From the very beginning he is destined for this. "Sacrifice and offering Thou didst not desire, but Thou hast prepared a body for me; in holocausts and sin-offerings Thou didst not delight. Then I said, 'Behold I come, as it is written of me in the scroll; I have come, O God, to do Thy will.' "

The will of the Father, as is clear from the context, is to manifest his love to all mankind. Here we see constantly the oneness of Christ's love for the Father and his all-embracing love for his brethren, which glorifies the Father. Therefore, the Father has glorified him, has made him Lord and Redeemer of the whole world.

The *Constitution on the Church in the Modern World*, Article 24, explains the meaning of redeemed personalism in the perspective of the Lord's prayer to the Father "that all may be one as We are one." This opens vistas beyond the reach of human reason, for it implies a certain likeness between the union of the Divine Persons and the union of God's sons and daughters in truth and charity. This likeness reveals that man, "who is the only creature on earth which God willed for itself, cannot fully find his true self except through a sincere giving of himself."

Christ is the risen Lord, the glorified Lord, whose victory of love was achieved in his human nature through his total giving of self. In the heavenly liturgy, he, the man, is raised up to "the right hand of the Father" in concelebration of the divine triune love. This is the glory of the humanity of Christ as head of redeemed mankind, the perfect personality, the one who has fully preserved his uniqueness, his self-respect in self-surrender, according to the mission the Father bestowed on him for all his brethren.

THE CHRISTIAN CONCEPT OF VIRTUE: OPENNESS

The paschal mystery is not something apart from God's love; it is the very revelation of his love. The Father glorifies the human nature of Christ, who makes himself a servant of his brethren, washing their feet, giving humble service, surrendering himself as ransom for them; and in an unlimited sense he is anointed with the Spirit and filled with joy. His glory is to communicate this same joy and love to his disciples, breaking all the obstacles which self-centeredness has brought into man's world.

It is in this context that we must understand the genuine Christian concept of virtue. (It may be that we shall have to look for another word, because "virtue" means widely different things depending on the various forms of personalism.)

According to the ethics of the Stoics and the philosophy of Aristotle and others, man's chief concern should be to perfect himself for his own glory, to enjoy his own perfection. He accepts and fosters a certain order—justice, temperance, and so on—but chiefly out of concern for this self-fulfillment.

The Christian concept is different. Virtue and self-fulfillment can never be achieved by a selfish concern for satisfaction. Virtue comes only through man's openness to the Other; it comes on the shoulders of solidarity, love, service. In loving concern for the others, we are and become truly ourselves. The paschal mystery emphatically teaches us this truth. But has it always shaped our ideas of Christian ethics?

The authors of manuals have not always taught this Christian concept so clearly and completely. Until recently they had a predilection for complicated formulas, like the one from medieval scholastic theology about a man on a bridge who sees a fellow man in the waves below about to drown at any moment. The question was posed: May you risk your life to help him? The first response of St. Thomas Aquinas and other Aristotelian theologians was that *per se* it is not allowed, because it would be against the rule of personalism enunciated in the Bible, whereby you have to love yourself more than others.

St. Thomas's reasoning was that, in the Bible's command to "love your neighbor as yourself," the love of others is compared to your self-love; therefore, self-love is the original part (as Aristotle also said) and it would not be the just balance of virtue to love one's neighbor as much as one's self or even more. But being Christians, these theologians had to extricate themselves from this reasoning and find an answer more favorable to Christian action. The sophisticated solution was: If you dive into the waves you do it chiefly not for the poor fellow but, in the final analysis, for your own progress in virtue, and by means of this well-ordered intention you gain merits and eternal reward for yourself; thus you observe the rule of love by loving yourself before your neighbor. After complicated reasoning of this sort, you may now virtuously save your neighbor—provided he has managed to stay afloat during the long reasoning process! But even then this kind of motivation will not bring home the reward of unselfish love.

The rule of "love your neighbor as yourself" has been revealed by Christ's own sacrifice and by his words, "No one has greater love than the one who gives his life for his friends" (John 15:13). He gave his life for sinners, making them his friends. It follows that in a Christlike personalism "none of us lives to himself and none of us dies to himself. If we live, we live to the Lord, and if we die, we die to the Lord" (Rom. 14:8).

In some ascetical works of the last century, we find another distortion of "virtue," especially the virtue of charity, in a tendency to gaze from on high on the poor and unfortunate as offering an opportunity—an "occasion"—to increase one's own checking account of merits. But anyone helped materially by such charity will feel humbled by the thought that he is, after all, just a good "occasion" for the "virtuous" man to exalt himself.

How different is all this from the biblical picture of the merciful Samaritan! He did not calculate how much he might gain from the business of helping the man who had fallen into the hands of the robbers. The robbers had left him nothing, but the Samaritan put their victim on his own horse, brought him to the hospital, and paid the bill. There was no reckoning of virtue, merit, or gain here. On the contrary, we find here the whole splendor and real fulfillment of true virtue and law: the manifestation of an outgoing and saving love.

5

THE BODY IN A PERSONALISTIC OUTLOOK

THE Epistle to the Hebrews explains the fundamental mission and prayer of Christ by pointing to the reality of his body. The Word Incarnate is the bodily presence and nearness of God to man. He redeems us in his body and with his blood. Therefore, his whole life says to the Father, "Thou hast prepared a body for me . . . Behold I come, O God, to do Thy will" (Heb. 10:5-7).

In this biblical passage, "body" means almost the same thing as "human nature." We can even dare to say that the body and blood of Christ really bring us in touch with God's saving love. Hence the body has an important significance in Christianity.

PERSONS OR SOULS

St. Augustine uses the expression "God and my soul" to describe the essence of religion. But this phrase has a Greek

43

connotation. It does not express the full relationship between the Christian person and God in the covenant, sealed by the blood of Christ. The personalism manifested by Christ in the paschal mystery has to do not only with his soul. Christ did not come to free his soul from his body or to redeem our souls from our bodies. He offers his body, glorifies the Father through it, and the glory of the Father shines upon it.

Christ is fully man, a person in a body, the Word Incarnate. So Christian personalism can never accept the view of Plato and other Greek philosophers who considered the body as a prison of the soul. Christianity honors the body fashioned by God, rejoices in it, respects its powers and its passions and purifies them through wisdom and love.

The concept of a passionless, "pious" Christian is a Hellenistic one, not a Christian concept. The Stoic was taught not to reveal any passion, sorrow, joy, or compassion. His ideal was the passionless soul—*ataraxia*. The ideal person was unmoved, especially unmoved by joy, love, or compassion. This type of thinking—although somewhat modified—found its way into the rules of certain religious congregations which held, for instance, that one of the great faults—at least a venial sin—is loud laughter! Thomas Aquinas, and along with him the monastic ascetical tradition, quoted Aristotle to the effect that there must be *castigatio vocis,* control of the voice, especially with respect to laughter.

The rules of some religious houses overemphasized the importance of self-control and of purely spiritual acts of intellect and will to such an extent that the personal reality of the body—contemplation by means of all five senses, the human energy of the passions in the service of the good—could not be fully appreciated. In order to preserve the "supernatural" quality of love, ascetical and scholastic theology often displayed a suspicious attitude toward any passionate, strong, fully human form of love. Even today, in some religious quarters, the effects of this Greek heritage can be seen in an all too disembodied attitude toward love and charity.

For the Greek, love was *eros* which, according to our own way of thinking, also finds expression in the passions of our whole being, soul *and* body. According to Greek thought, *eros* was not considered primarily a passion, however, but chiefly a matter of lofty ideas of self-perfection and will. Imagine love as something confined only to the intellect and will!

For the Stoic the passions and emotions indeed had some relation to the fullness of virtue, but only to the extent that they were perfectly repressed by the will and by purely spiritual-intellectual contemplation.

PASSION AND COMPASSION

The life and death of Christ present us with a completely different picture, however. In Him we see the loving brother and totally consecrated Son. His whole life is compassion, concern for others, and passionate dedication. People experience his goodness and sincerity with amazement, awe, and joy. At the Last Supper, in the upper room, every word of his conversation with his friends is a message of love, human and divine. For the apostles it was an experience they could never forget. "It was there from the beginning; we have heard it, we have seen it with our own eyes; we looked upon it and felt it with our own hands; it is of this we tell" (I John 1:1). Christ is capable of the keenest suffering; he weeps at the grave of Lazarus. On the cross, bearing the frustration of his brethren, he cries in agony, "My God, why hast Thou forsaken me?" Yet, in the midst of his own suffering, he consoles his mother and has words of compassion for the thief at his side. He is a person of great passion, but everything is an expression of his passionate love for the heavenly Father and his brethren.

The introduction to the *Constitution on the Church in the Modern World* begins with *"Gaudium et spes"*: "The joy and hope, the anguish and sorrow of our brethren are also ours." Christ shares all joy, sorrow, hope, anguish, and makes it manifest in his body and in his whole life. The hope of Christian personalism is therefore not just beatitude for the soul; it is the full splendor of God's love and brotherhood for the body as well. The body is a word, a message, a bridge, open, vulnerable, and glorious, if the love is right and if it is respectful and unselfish. Therefore, at the end of all things, the bodies of those who are in God's love will be glorious in the communion of saints with the risen Christ.

THE RESURRECTION OF THE BODY, AND ETHICS

Numerous Catholics, and even more Protestants, think of the assumption of the Blessed Virgin Mary, body and soul into heaven, as just an extra bit of devotion, an utterly useless dogma. I do not share this view. The dogma does not separate the Blessed Virgin from the communion of saints; it expresses our hope for the full redemption of the body. I think it is an essential expression of the mystery of redemption that she who embodies the Church and is the prototype of the Church represents also the fullness of our Christian hope, which is not for the beatitude of separated souls alone but for our whole body "to be set free" (Rom. 8:23). We are redeemed in our body as well.

This perspective of Christian hope should determine our attitude toward the bodily reality on earth, and has great importance for our ideas about morality, especially in matters concerning the fifth and sixth commandments. Respect for health, dedication to the service of brethren, a genuine care and cult of the body in view of Christ's humanity, and even a sexual ethic are expressions of respect for the bodies of self and of others. Since God manifests his glory in the body of man, man has to glorify God in his own body.

Many Church Fathers thought that Christ, when he ascended to glory, was accompanied by all the saints of Israel and of the holy people who lived before him. The glory of his body shines in the glory of their bodies. If this is an acceptable theological concept, then it is consistent that his mother, who was so closely associated with the mystery of the incarnation, cannot be expected to be a "separated soul," leading a kind of bodiless existence.

With this view so deeply rooted in the Bible and in the ancient tradition, I dare to express it as my personal opinion that none of us who are in Christ will have to wait as a "separated soul" for a redeemed body until the Parousia of the Lord at the end of history. I think that those who are perfected in God's love will share bodily in the glory of the risen Lord: that they will receive a risen body fitting the degree of holiness they have attained at the end of their period of purification. "What we now sow is not the body that shall be" (I Cor. 15:37). What we shall be will manifest the love we are now sowing in this bodily existence. It is not only our soul that has a share in Christ's redemption. Even in this life, in the body of Christ's friends, there shines forth kindness, goodness, respect, and purity. Yet these things are only a symbol and a beginning of what we are hoping for.

In the fourteenth century there was an interesting dispute between the theologians of the time and Pope John XXII (1316-1334), who repeatedly preached and taught that the separated souls will not enjoy the beatific vision until the Parousia of the Lord. In a gathering at the University of Paris, the theologians censured him, and a commission of cardinals persuaded the Pope to correct some of his views. In his bull *Ne super his* of December 3, 1334, the Pope declared: "We desire to be considered as not having said whatever in our words is not in agreement with the Catholic faith, the teaching of the church, Holy Scripture or good custom; we condemn it and submit everything that we have said or written on this matter to the decision of the Church and of my successors" (Denzinger-Schönmetzer, No. 991). But Pope John XXII and the theologians were perhaps both partially right and partially wrong, each emphasizing one aspect of the truth: Pope John by insisting that it is not separated souls but persons in the body who come to final fulfillment, and the theologians by insisting that the final fulfillment of the saints will not be delayed until the longed-for Parousia of the Lord. Thus, those who rejoice in the peace of the Lord after death will not be blessed "separated souls" according to the Greek or Stoic view, released from the prison of the body, but rather persons who have reached the fullness of being in a new form, including the redemption of the body. After death—after final purification—we will find ourselves in that body which will be the reward for our genuine personalism on earth and which will be manifest to the whole world at the coming of the Lord.

A number of Catholic and Protestant theologians to whom I have explained these ideas think that they are capable of shedding new light on the dogma of the assumption of Mary "in body and soul." The uniqueness of her role in the history of redemption is not diminished, but neither is she severed from the communion of saints; her privileges in the communion of saints appear more clearly. Thus the dogma liberates our Christian hope for ourselves from any tendency to disregard the body, and it causes us to glorify God in our bodies. It is a message of salvation and a call to wholeness for all.

THE BODY AS A SIGN OF PRESENCE

Christians cannot look upon the body as a secondary thing. We must reject any view that depreciates it as a prison of the soul, or as an object owned by the soul, or an embodiment of sinfulness. Christ, the Word Incarnate, was not separated into two disparate units. His life and his sacrificial death and resurrection assign full value to the body and emphasize the great opportunity to render glory to God through the body. Is it not specifically his body, as a sign of his saving presence in the world, that he gave us for a remembrance: the body that worked, healed, suffered, saw his neighbor's needs, and spilled its blood to tell the world about his love and the love of the Father?

The mystery of the incarnation, death, and resurrection of Christ obliges us to develop a personalistic ethics of the body, centered on the love of God. Love has to be expressed on all levels, and this means among other things a redeemed outlook about sex—an understanding and appreciation of a sexuality totally integrated in the love taught by Christ, which redeems man in all his dimensions.

It means also that we must see our body as something indispensable to spiritual action. By virtue of it we become present and accessible to our fellow man, informed about his needs, able to communicate with him and respond to him. We shake hands as a sign of friendship, and we turn our countenance to others. And if our heart is right, our body, along with our innermost being, will also turn to God and neighbor. Thus, we can share with each other, visibly and actually, gentleness, joy, sorrow, compassion, hope, and all the other mediations of love.

Because of this, we will assign greater importance to all visible things—the evolution of the universe, means of communication, expressions of art, and all the transformation of material things which makes them capable of rendering service to mankind. Such a perspective will preserve us from having a merely utilitarian outlook toward the visible world and a merely materialistic one toward our bodily energies.

This perspective of personalism also has its cosmic dimensions. The history and dynamism of hundreds of millions of years in the evolutionary process find their culmination in the body of the human person. Indeed, the whole universe is yearning to be freed from the shackles of mortality. In the resurrection of Christ and of all those who accept redemption from him, the visible world receives its crown and fulfillment. The whole universe is involved in our hope for resurrection. It waits with us "for God to set our whole body free" (Rom. 8:23).

6

PERSONALISM AND
SELF-FULFILLMENT

I N THE specific I-Thou-We personalism of the paschal mys-
tery, we are fully aware that we owe our being-a-person to
the one who calls us and who calls us all together. We find
our true self when we respond to him and entrust our self
to him who is the Rallying Call, the living God, the Thou. And
we know that we are being most faithful to our own self—
we can be best "fulfilled"—by being faithful to him and thus
to our calling to love one another in him.

It makes some difference whether we speak about a voca-
tion to perfection or a calling to holiness, and even more
difference what we understand by these terms.

Holiness is a thoroughly religious concept. It has to do with
worship, is praise of the one who alone is holy, gratitude
for the splendor of his goodness. Yet the word can be mis-
understood and its message distorted, for example, by speaking
about "self-sanctification," which by its emphasis on man's
own achievement conceals God's gracious action in him.

The true meaning of the biblical word *teleios,* which we translate as "perfect," is complete openness to the fullness of the manifestation of God's saving love. Unfortunately, the English word does not convey this full idea very well. As used today, the word "perfection" implies an exaggerated self-consciousness; and we know that the Bible violently assails those who consider themselves perfect in this sense.

Here I shall approach the idea of self-fulfillment from various angles in order to distinguish the genuine human, Christian concept of self-fulfillment in the perspective of holiness from the self-centered idea of "fulfillment" which is more a self-conscious satisfaction than true fulfillment of self.

GOD'S HOLINESS AND MAN'S DEVELOPMENT

God alone is perfect; he alone is the Holy One. The Sermon on the Mount leads to this crowning thought: "Be therefore perfect just as your heavenly Father is perfect" (Matt. 5:48). These words are often misunderstood or misused. If we want to understand a biblical text, we must always see it in context. Here we find that, in his infinite "perfection," God loves even his enemies, namely sinners. He acts compassionately by sending rain and sunshine to the wicked and the good. He is patient. He forgives, and by this reconciling graciousness, he calls man to conversion, growth, and the fullness of love and life. The Bible tells us nothing about a lonely God who cares only for his own perfection; it speaks of a God who manifests himself as holy by his goodness and saving kindness, shown even to sinners.

The New English Bible rightly translates "Be perfect" as "Be all goodness, just as your heavenly Father is all good." St. Luke, in his shortened version of the Sermon on the Mount (we call it the Sermon on the Plain), says, "Be compassionate as your heavenly Father is compassionate" (Luke 6:36).

The difference in wording between the Sermon on the Mount and the Sermon on the Plain is interesting. We have the same message, but presented according to different images and concepts. St. Matthew reveals Christ preaching to the crowd on a mount, while Luke says: "He went down the hill with them and took His stand on the level ground" (Luke 6:17). He meets the crowd where they wait for him. Why, then, does St. Matthew place Christ on the mountain? He was expressing the same truth, but according to another image— the Old Testament image of Moses, who alone on the top of Mount Sinai received the tablets of the Law. Matthew's listeners were Jews, people familiar with the Old Testament, so he represented Christ as going up the mountain with his disciples, not alone like Moses, but as the Emmanuel who is close to all, to the whole crowd of people. Luke, on the other hand, was preaching to Greeks who did not know anything about the story of Mount Sinai. To them the mountain would have no significance. So Luke used the image of Christ going down to the plain with the crowd: Christ, or *God,* among us. He conveys the same message of God's ineffable holiness and his nearness to men. What strikes us in both accounts is that the concepts of God's holiness and perfection are associated with his mercy, compassion, nearness to man. We have a message of God's outgoing (revealing) love.

In the Old Testament, the great theme of God's holiness is treated, in the context of mercy, as the real goal of his justice. The following text of Hosea (11:9), for example, is classical: "I will not return to destroy Ephraim, because I am God and not man: the Holy One in the midst of you."

Man can be called perfect or holy insofar as he experiences God's saving justice and mercy. If he speaks of "self-sanctification" or perfection in a self-centered way, he becomes most unholy; he is placing himself in opposition to God's holiness and to his undeserved love and mercy.

When we pray "Hallowed be Thy name," we pray not that we may give something to God but that in his compassionate love he may give us renewed grace to praise him, the Holy One, in his love and kindness. Thus, we see God's own action revealing the splendor of his love, and we respond, aware that everything is by his grace and not by our own merit. We honor his holy name by mutual love, mercy, compassion, and respect.

CONSECRATED FOR SERVICE AND LOVE

God's holiness and perfection is revealed in the Messiah, the Anointed One, Christ. In the Bible he is often called "the Holy One," which means that in his human nature he is totally consecrated for service, anointed by the Spirit to bring good news to the poor, and thus to be the servant of Yahweh in his all-embracing goodness.

The biblical meaning of "consecration" and "sanctification" often is that God takes hold of a man and sends him to be his voice, his witness, his dedicated servant. He calls the prophets, cleanses them, and sends them out to proclaim and do his will. Their basic experience is the authority of the holy God. See, for example, the vision of Isaiah. The shattering experience of his own unworthiness *follows* God's purifying action and mission. "One of the seraphim flew to me; in his hands was a live coal which he had taken with the tongs off the altar. He touched my mouth and said, 'Behold this has touched your lips and your iniquities shall be taken away and your sin shall be cleansed.' Then I heard the voice of the Lord, 'Whom shall I send?' And I said, 'Lo, here am I. Send me' " (Isaiah 6:3-8).

As Christ, the Anointed One, is consecrated by the Spirit for his redemptive mission, so he consecrates his disciples by the same power of the Spirit. "Consecrate them in truth. Thy word is truth. As Thou hast sent me into the world and for their sake, I now consecrate myself that they too may be consecrated in truth" (John 17:17-19). Consecration by Christ liberates the disciples from self-concern and egotism. It includes a call to oneness for the honor of the one who is holy. "The glory which Thou gavest me, I have given to them that they may be one, as we are one; I in them and Thou in me, may they be perfected to oneness, then will the world learn that Thou didst send me" (John 17:22-23).

This same transformation of a man by God's sanctifying action is marvelously expressed in the Gospel of St. John where Christ tells Peter, who has confessed his triple denial, that he will be sent and will go where he does not wish to go, and will glorify God. It is a final sign that Peter is consecrated, that he will finally go "where he had no wish to go" (John 21:19). This is quite a challenging text for certain frustrated priests, brothers, nuns, and laymen who have dedicated their life to "self-fulfillment." Their frustration really arises from their self-consciousness, which prevents them from accepting their real mission. The truly consecrated person gives up his own desires and follows the divine mission. He is sent and he goes. He is consecrated, like Christ, who "did not come to please Himself" (Rom. 15:3).

True Christian personalism means that a person is sanctified who accepts God's grace and calling, consecrates himself as a servant to service, witness, and love, and no longer seeks principally his own self-fulfillment. Nevertheless, or rather because of this, he will find the greatest possible fulfillment in life.

GOD'S GRACIOUSNESS AND MAN'S CALL TO HOLINESS

Christian holiness must not be understood from the viewpoint of human effort, success, or glory, as Pelagius held. The Christian biblical understanding of holiness means a life in conformity with the sanctifying action of God. The perspective is that of a God loving us, showing us by his gifts, by the needs of others revealed to us, and by the operations of the Holy Spirit, what his design is for us. Sanctity means that we conform our life to this grace, fully accepting God's action in and around us as the norm of our life.

Holiness is life conformed to grace, but we must clearly understand what grace is. It is not something added externally to our nature as persons, but it is God's gracious action within us which makes us aware that he is with us. The awesome and joyous awareness of this transforms our egocentric being ("un-nature") so that we have a new outlook, characterized by gratitude, love, returning to him what is really his own, giving glory to him, and rendering service to his brethren. Thus, what we are and what we have is transformed into "grace," if we in turn render everything to him and use it in the service of his family.

Just as we warn that an unhealthy concern for self-fulfillment cannot be reconciled with the biblical vision of holiness as a response to God's graciousness, so must we also warn against any form of asceticism that on the practical level disregards the gifts of God to the person.

Respect for God's gifts is a rule particularly for church leaders and also for rulers in the secular world. Grace does not belittle nature. We must not disregard the Creator's gifts to the person in order to magnify the grace of the Redeemer. God is both Creator and Redeemer; one God gives us his Holy Spirit and all other gifts. Through his grace we appreciate them as signs of his love and use them for his glory.

Any attempt to stifle the nature of a person—that is, those natural qualities which are God's gifts—inevitably leads to a vehement concern for self-fulfillment. This can mean a firm decision not to allow anyone to bury our talents in the earth; but it can—as a reaction—degenerate into a frustrating self-consciousness and self-concern. When, on the other hand, those in authority show respect for the particular talents and capabilities of individuals, and thus bring home all the wealth of God's gifts for the common good, it becomes easier for everyone to offer his service and to use to the utmost his opportunities for the good of all. Thus God's "grace" is made manifest.

For the sake of God's glory or grace, we cannot forgo the use of any of our capabilities. Everything we are and everything we have is a precious gift of God for his praise and the service of our brethren. Occasionally, however, for the sake of our brethren, it is advisable for us to forget some special talent or renounce the development of some particular capability if the community needs another kind of service more. For instance, I thought that during my wartime medical service I had developed a real professional interest and some skill and joy in what I was doing. But this did not mean that after years in the service I was obliged to concentrate on this special talent or interest. A person should renounce, and even must renounce, any particular pleasure, even an important service, if God calls him to another kind of service, such as to preach the Gospel. Thus, there are times when we are not permitted to exploit all our particular talents, but we must always employ to the fullest extent those which are in accordance with the real needs of the community, the people of God. This will bring us genuine self-fulfillment. If, on the contrary, we decide out of self-concern to use only what is best for our own exaltation, we will ultimately be frustrated. But if we offer to serve according to the best of our capabilities, we will enjoy a life of fulfillment.

ONENESS AND HOLINESS

All aspects of salvation and holiness are summed up in God's saving love, which makes men able to love each other for the glory of his name. "God is holy" means the same as "God is love." From all eternity, the Father expresses his infinite love in his Word, the Son, and the Word is love, united to the Father in the Holy Spirit. This Spirit of Holiness, Spirit of Love, consecrates Christ's human nature for his mission to manifest the full extent of God's love. So holiness is a calling to love and to love together, a calling to oneness, to solidarity. One of the oldest eucharistic prayers in the Oriental liturgy concludes all the invocations with the following unifying petition: "Lord, make us one; lead us to holiness."

FULFILLMENT IN SACRIFICE AND LOVE

We must constantly be reminded that Christ made possible the whole sanctifying mission of the Church—love and unity—through his sacrifice. Through his redemptive life-death sacrifice, he has abolished all ritual sacrifices and all kinds of merely ritual priesthood. Christ has offered himself as a total disclosure of his love for his Father and his brethren. The eucharist and other sacraments, therefore, do not bring us closer to salvation by means of mere ritualism. They are an undeserved calling to follow Christ in this existential way, by devoting ourselves, our capabilities, and all we possess to our brothers, and doing away with whatever prevents us from realizing this kind of sacrificial love which Christ has manifested. We celebrate the mystery of faith truly if we accept it as a rule of our life, a rule which we can follow only through God's grace.

Looking at the ideal of self-perfection now in this perspective, we see that it has a genuine meaning only if we are convinced that we can find true self-fulfillment—the fulfillment of our true self—in humble love, greeting not only those who greet us, as the heathen do (Matt. 5:47), and loving not only those who love us, but praising God, giving him honor by goodness and kindness toward those who insult us or misunderstand us.

We come to fullness of being only through faith and grace. To those who believe, God shows his saving justice and his gracious mercy by justifying sinners. When he manifests his compassionate love by forgiveness for us, he bestows on us a mission to be instruments of peace for others. Thus, the peace and joy of the Lord comes to fullness in us and through us.

Because of his consecration for his brethren, Christ manifests his glory and his "fulfillment" in his resurrection. We too, out of appreciation for the great gift of our calling which God has bestowed upon us, should consecrate our service, ministry, and all our energies by conforming our life to his sanctifying action. Fulfillment, and finally, a share in the glory of the risen Lord, will follow inevitably. The less self-concerned we are, the greater will be our experience of the beatitudes even here on earth.

THE SELF-RESPECT AND UNIQUENESS OF THE PERSON

Although fulfillment is found ultimately in unselfish love, this always includes *self-respect*. We must not demean ourselves. We have to empty ourselves as far as pride and vanity are concerned, but we must respect God, who calls us to uniqueness with his unique gifts. He wants us to be something more than mere instruments; we have to make a contribution as persons with healthy self-respect, humility, and dignity in the sight of God, and with an eye to the singularity of our calling and the authenticity of our response.

The I-Thou-We relationship cannot be realized if we give up our own individuality. If we are not our own self and do not live according to our own conscience, we cannot contribute to or enrich other persons. Christ, the head of redeemed mankind, is the perfect personality, the one who has fully preserved identity, uniqueness, and full self-respect in self-surrender. So the I-Thou-We relationship in authentic love means the fulfillment of our true self, achieved in openness, gratitude, and communication.

Christ's witness of true love is his glory, the ultimate fulfillment, and he reveals to all persons the way toward a genuine self-fulfillment. This demands, of course, self-denial, but a self-denial destructive only of selfishness, not of our true self. Unfortunately, this has often not been properly understood.

7

OPTIONS FOR SOCIAL ORGANIZATION

Pierre Teilhard de Chardin was a Christian personalist in the truest sense. His vision, inspired by deep meditation and mystical experience, was an effective answer to the accusation that religion estranges man from the world. He looked on the whole universe as praise of God the Creator of all things. Man, and man's decisions, constituted the principal evidence for him of the evolutionary process on earth. Salvation history meant the development of an ever-keener awareness by men of the presence of God and greater acknowledgment that he is the one who guides us.

Teilhard's passionate love for the universe is personalistic and existential. All his spiritual sensitivity, compassion, and love of mankind, as well as his scientific attainments, were directed toward his life goal of explaining, for the benefit of men today, his vision of one continuous creation, one order of salvation, and one long pilgrimage of men together to God. He wanted us to be urgently aware of the crisis of

59

choice that must now be faced by "planetized humanity," and he was deeply concerned that men should recognize both the great dangers and tremendous opportunities in the options open to them at the present moment.

The first reaction to any ideal of a totalized humanity— and Teilhard understood this very well—is usually revulsion, due to fear of depersonalization. We think of slavery and of the brutalizing techniques commonly employed in most political collectivisms; and we fear not only the loss of personal freedom but the loss to the world of the unique contribution of each individual. We may be tempted, momentarily, to consider retreating to the kind of individualism that has possessed us too long, or to seek refuge behind the ramparts of nationalism or racial tribalism.

But reality must be faced; it is there and it cannot be re- versed. It becomes for us a dialogue with God, who speaks through the events of world history. He speaks; but because he has created man in freedom, the decisions are man's— alone—to make. As Christians, what must our responsibility for these decisions be? What decisions are in conformity with the Gospel? Do hope and understanding impel us to social commitment? To what kind of social solutions should we be committed, and what kind of philosophies and structures will best serve these goods?

Upon deeper reflection, we do indeed see great dangers both threatening and challenging a humanity that now is spread over the surface of the earth. Above all, and beyond these things, we see a convergence of unifying forces so marvelous that we must recognize it as the presence of the Lord of his- tory manifesting the goal toward which he is beckoning us.

One of these converging forces is a certain tendency to form groups and organizations, which is at the very core of the evolutionary process and which permeates all life. This tendency emerges psychically in man and operates through interpersonal communication and action in ever-larger and more complex groupings: in family, tribe, commune, state, nation, and now in certain kinds of global organizations.

Of itself, therefore, totalization poses no threat, but rather offers us the hope of a new evolutionary impetus toward a more mature humanity and toward persons made more effective as a result of universal intercommunication and interaction. Yet the concrete planning for totalization rests with men's decisions, and it is on this, therefore, that our concern, attention, and efforts must be concentrated. Depersonalization *can* come about through certain types of imposed collectivization; fragmentation and eventual dissolution *can* result from self-centered individualism. But, if structures are built with a view to persons and their freedoms and responsibilities, we can also witness great strides along the road to wholeness of persons and humanity. Structures will become useful and effective if they reflect a personalistic attitude toward human life, work, society, and organization.

Vatican Council II's *Constitutions on the Church* place great emphasis on the dignity and freedom of each individual person and on the duty of the community and society to respect and protect this dignity and freedom by means of proper social, economic, and political structures. But the council also stressed the reciprocal nature of this duty: the individual person also has a duty to contribute toward the building of proper structures in community and society. It is of the utmost importance, therefore, for the Christian world to emphasize, both in its teaching and in its practice, how highly it regards responsible personal liberty, a responsibility accepted in communion with others and for the sake of the community, not simply for the personal welfare of the individual.

COLLECTIVISM

One of the worst enemies of personalism is collectivism, an ideology that hopes to achieve ultimate goals—political, social, or economic—through the use of naked power. Organization aims at the successful use of power, instead of service to a community by a community. Communism assumed this form under Stalin and Mao Tse-tung. The process led inevitably to the formation of oppressive power structures and resulted in a depersonalized and depersonalizing economy and a society that allowed little leeway for liberty and individual responsibility.

There are other philosophies which advocate a similarly impersonal approach but with a view toward some form of social personalism. Such was the liberalism of Adam Smith and David Ricardo, both of whom greatly influenced the thinking of Karl Marx. They held that the economic order is autonomous and must follow its own laws without regard for ethical considerations. Economists operate according to economic norms without regard for moral demands or consideration for service to individuals or to other areas of social life. In the political field, Machiavelli espoused the same thought, denying the right of moralists to moralize about politics, because politics is the art of power. The basis for this approach was an optimism that economic or political progress would of itself work for the best interests of man.

We have now reached a stage in the history of mankind where it is clear that such economics and politics can destroy man. It can bring about the kind of impersonalism described in the milieu theory of Auguste Comte and Émile Durkheim. We, of course, recognize the great influence which environment has on human behavior and human thought, but to recognize this influence is not the same thing as declaring that man, in his whole personality and in his conscience, is only the product of a passive adjustment to environment.

The thinking of Karl Marx must be assessed in the light of this scientific search for the determining factor in man's environment. He believed that the development of the economy determines what man will be, since economics determines the environment and environment shapes man. Other factors, such as state, culture, religion, morality, he regarded as mere superstructures of economic relationships.

We do Marx an injustice, however, if we overemphasize his scientific approach (which eventually defeated his underlying personalistic intention) and fail to understand that unjust economic structures did indeed condemn many men of the lower working class to an unworthy kind of life, making them unable to enjoy freedom and reach maturity. The young Karl Marx especially was imbued with a prophetic fervor for the dignity of man. He saw how the structures of economic life affected man's mode of living, and he protested against the exploitation of persons. He deeply desired to bring about economic relationships and structures that would help preserve and promote the dignity of man.

No one would claim that Marx proposed an existentialism, but he did raise questions that demanded existentialistic answers; and despite his impersonal approach, there are many personalistic aspects about his thought. He brings together, even if not in good harmony, the great prophetic traditions of the Old Testament and the ethics of concern for all men, especially those of the lowest classes. So, apart from his formulation of dialectical materialism, we must recognize his real personalistic intention, even though he defeats it by his naïve assumption that a final synthesis of perfect relationships could be brought about through increasing conflict or class warfare.

In its concrete realization, communism has not turned out as Karl Marx visualized it. Its aggressive ideology and oppressive emphasis on administration has resulted in an almost total loss of personal liberty. Yet communism and socialism could embark on a different course. There is the possibility— and history proves it—that beyond such totalitarian frameworks there can develop a prophetic hope for the wholeness of man and for improved personal relationships in an economy directed toward the benefit of man.

Before Marx, Ferdinand Lassalle, the leader of early socialism in Germany, advocated much more social personalism, an absolute concern for the dignity of man in economic and social life. Lassalle felt strongly that the dignity of man in community was threatened by the excessive individualism of the possessive class and by its insistence on clinging to its own privileges, wealth, and power. He advocated the establishment of new forms of economic structure, with shared ownership, shared participation, and shared responsibility.

Lassalle was in touch with Bishop Ketteler of Mainz, who, before the Communist Manifesto in 1848, issued fervent appeals for reform in his social speeches but was insulted or ignored by many of his co-officials in the Church. The difference between Lassalle and Ketteler, who were friends (Lassalle was a believer but not a Catholic), was chiefly in the matter of implementation. Ketteler thought that an appeal made out of deep faith and with great conviction, an appeal which all men could understand, would lead people spontaneously to see that the working class must have a share in responsibility and ownership. Lassalle said this was naïve romanticism: that laws and interference by the state were necessary to bring this about.

Populorum Progressio, the social encyclical of Pope Paul VI, reflects much of Ketteler's thought but even more of Lassalle's realism. We have learned in the meantime that enthusiasm alone is not enough; appropriate legislation is also necessary. This elemental fact must still be learned by many of the "younger breed" who want personalism without legislation and structures. They are right, however, in protesting against oppressive or unreasonable structures.

Some of these wishful thinkers have actually wandered from the straight path, seeking a new form of Christianity without institutions. But a genuine redeemed personalism, a true I-Thou-*We* personalism, acknowledges the necessity of institutions on earth. We have to endure not only the imperfections of our own selves but those of institutions as well. This means further struggle between the I-centered, unredeemed approach and the redeemed approach will go on with a constant need for conversion and a constant need for the renewal of institutions through personal initiative.

One of our greatest tasks today is to come to a balanced view about shared responsibility and spontaneous initiative, and to provide structures that promote both these ideals. The fundamental approach of Christian doctrine with respect to social life—namely emphasis on love and social justice—means that Christians must be devoted to a harmonized renewal of mind and heart and reform of structures. Both aspects must be stressed; they must meet and foster each other.

The renewal of our thinking is neither earnest nor realistic if it does not find new expressions and does not embody this thinking in new structures. Moreover, even the reform of structures will fail if the way is not prepared by a constant effort at community education. We can see this on all levels and in all societies; the Church is no exception. Consider the case of liturgical reform. It is not enough for a priest to observe the new rules unless he also thoroughly absorbs the whole conciliar and post-conciliar way of thinking about the liturgy and helps people to understand the new formulas.

The council was very much concerned that all the faithful, including even the simplest, should clearly understand that the liturgy is intended to be the proclamation of the good news, a communication among the people of God, an intelligent praise of God. For everybody it should be an expression of life in community, preparing him for life in the community outside of the liturgical celebration. When this is understood, something else becomes clear: the new forms and structures are intended to express God's dynamic presence in the Church and the world for all times. If this message is not communicated in ways understandable to our own age, and if structures do not allow for adequate spontaneity, tensions will inevitably erupt.

It is true that progress never comes about without tension, but the tensions can become unhealthy if we do not try to harmonize the two aspects: thought and renewal of structures. Members of the Church should profit from experience in the political and social fields which recognizes that both these aspects must be respected. Not only is any proclamation of a new law doomed to failure if public opinion and convictions are not prepared for it in advance, but, conversely, convictions and public opinion can give rise to great tensions if they are not incorporated, as far as possible, in new structures and new ways of life.

INDIVIDUALISM

Marxism accused Christianity and all religion of alienating man from his earthly task, and in the nineteenth century there was enough truth in this accusation to make it credible. One of the causes of collectivism must be acknowledged to be reaction against the extravagant individualism of so many Christians, including some of the most popular ascetical writers.

This individualism, which has come to the fore more and more in European thought ever since the thirteenth and fourteenth centuries, strongly influenced the *devotio moderna* of the fifteenth and sixteenth centuries. Even Thomas a Kempis's *Imitation of Christ,* the most classical and beautiful of such books, is marked by a notable individualism. We find in it no word about structures, no commitment to improve the world or promote brotherhood. Lesser devotional works, chiefly for pious women, admonished them on entering a church to "forget about everything around you . . . the concerns of your house, your husband and children have nothing to do with your prayers; it is only you, your soul, and God alone." And therefore when they left church, prayer did not go along with them into their lives; there was no genuine bridge from prayer to life.

With this individualistic thought permeating society, more and more Christians naturally concentrated on the one question: How can I gain God's mercy for *me;* how can I save *my own* soul? Philosophy and theology were remarkably unconcerned about universal matters, community, or structures. They considered only the individual soul, imprisoned in the body, and the world was looked upon as a prison for everyone. The only solution was to withdraw from the world and save one's own soul. In many cases, the reason for choosing religious life was that this was seen as the only or the easiest way to "save one's soul." We acknowledge, of course, the importance of saving one's soul; but our own salvation, if understood in this erroneous isolated way, promotes excessive individualism.

Individualism was reflected also in the field of Catholic moral theology. Many famous treatises about justice, especially those written since the seventeenth century, have little or nothing to say about social justice. They are concerned only with a type of commercial justice, an exchange between persons, between person and community. Christians could be devout, dedicated, pious people without having any sensitive social awareness. The glorification of God in the body had already been left out, as we have seen; now the whole community was left out.

This kind of so-called religion could not motivate any right kind of social or even religious commitment. It tended to alienate Christians from the world around them—or at least failed to cause them to act as Christians. We know how Karl Marx reacted; he called religion an alienation from life, something alienating man from society. Our response must be that this was not truly religion; it was this overemphasis on individualism that alienated man from the world.

After Napoleon's defeat, Europe witnessed not only the Holy Alliance between the emperors and kings of Russia, Prussia, Austria, the Bourbon kings, and the Papal States; it also saw the revival of a great deal of pre- or counter-revolutionary thought. In France, for example, Catholic thinkers advocated a school of thought called *l'ordre social,* marking a kind of return to the feudalism which had existed before the revolution. In many ways the Catholic outlook was regressive— a state of affairs that heightened the appeal of Karl Marx's dynamic social theory.

Marxism, on the contrary, offered a lively philosophy of history that attempted to show how humanity went through different phases in a dialectical process—thesis, antithesis and synthesis—and how tensions could be productive of progress. The dynamics of this philosophy appealed to European students who had already come to realize the irrelevance of an individualistic and static medieval outlook unrelated to their newer world.

The choice lay between Marxist philosophy and a static philosophy based on rational, immobile concepts and abstract ideas that were conditioned by past cultures. Many Catholic chairs in universities offered only this static philosophy, clothed in medieval dress, while the Marxists were advocating a philosophy of history which, although erroneous, appeared as something vital in contrast to these immobile concepts. In so doing, they took over something from our Christian heritage which we had not appreciated enough. For the Bible is not concerned with abstract philosophy; it is a history of salvation.

THE CONCILIAR APPROACH TO THE SOCIAL ORDER

The dynamic approach to life reflected in the recent council's documents now has made obsolete the social outlook characteristic of Catholic thought during the latter half of the nineteenth century, when Karl Marx was proclaiming his gospel. Compare the outlook of the French *ordre social* thinkers with Pope Paul's *Populorum Progressio*. The two words in the title, "people" and "progress," are a good illustration of the new approach. There is nothing about this document which resembles Lot's wife, who, on looking back, became immobile, a pillar of salt, a symbol for all subsequent reactionaries.

The documents of the Second Vatican Council reflect a biblical perspective and, at the same time, are a response to our own age. We Christians are not limited to bare, abstract philosophy; far from it. We are the ones who, with God, live the great history of salvation which has its center in the Redeemer of the world, the Word Incarnate. Thus, religion is not an estrangement from secular history; it encompasses secular history.

The conciliar directives on priestly training make it clear that their studies must begin with a fundamental treatment of the history of salvation in the light of the mystery of Christ. Likewise, the *Constitution on the Church in the Modern World* stresses the dynamic, absolutely serious consideration of the history, development, and progress of man. The Church has a mission to the men of all times. Of course, this does not invite naïve optimism that the progress of man is automatic; man must still make his own decisions and do his best. It means that God makes possible real progress if we listen to his voice and use present opportunities to shape the world for the benefit of man.

Christ promised us a concelebration of the love of the triune God, with and by the family of God, a sharing in the community of saints. And the way toward this is through the pilgrimage of all the people of God, the communion of saints on earth, solidarity with all people in all fields and on all levels. Our redemption resides in Christ's self-identification with his brethren, all of them, and we accept redemption by becoming active members of his mystical body in solidarity. There is no way of achieving the hope of brotherhood except through involvement in the cause of brotherhood on earth. This is the hope and understanding of the Church which motivates our social commitment.

We must not overlook the difference between this motivation, as proposed by the Second Vatican Council, and the motivation found in Harvey Cox's *Secular City*. Cox asserts that there is nothing in the heights or depths beyond the secular realm, and the only goal of his theology of hope seems to be the open future of this secular world. He does not specify whether or not there is something beyond this world. He does not exclude the idea of eternal life, but the doubt itself prompts a total interest in this world and its future. This "open future" may be called God, since it is doubtful that there is anything beyond. You dedicate all your energies to the one thing you know for sure, the secular city, and "believe" in it and its open future. Therefore, for Harvey Cox and other "secular" theologians, the real saint is a political saint, theological language is a political language, and our mission as Christians is to shape a better future here on earth. So the vanishing eschatological hope yields place to the hope for the secular city.

The real Christian motivation of our social commitment, on the other hand, is occasioned and conditioned by our eschatological hope, although this is not the narrow hope of separate individual souls living in lonely beatitude. The hope of the people of God—that they can concelebrate eternally the love of God—commits us to a here and now, because we are here put to the test. We cannot share this hope without sharing solidarity here on earth. And since the whole of mankind is redeemed, Christ is to be trusted and honored not only as the Redeemer of individual souls; he is honored as the Redeemer of the whole world by our response to the yearning of the world around us to experience the freedom and responsibility of the sons of God.

Christian hope motivates man in his wholeness or entirety, which means man in all his relationships and all his commitments. Hope expresses itself in these commitments. We cannot really believe in the salvation of man without doing our best to foster and preserve his wholeness in all its dimensions. This means a special awareness and responsibility on our part for all the forces that affect and shape man: culture, economy, politics, social and leisure life, which taken all together determine to a great extent man's further development or his disintegration.

Obviously, for genuine believers, this rules out the coziness of an individualistic I-Thou personalism built around a small community and interested only in personal fulfillment. It is certainly important to appreciate how vital these personalizing fundamental communities are in today's anonymous modern society, for it is from them that the consolidating and cooperating powers of love move out into the wider world. But, for this very reason, we cannot confine our interest to them. The couple, the family, the small community, must all reach out beyond themselves out of a desire for a deeper understanding of the world and their place in it.

This idea is explained at some length in the *Constitution on the Church in the Modern World* in the chapters dealing with the family, culture, economics, social progress, political action, and finally in the chapter on world peace and the development of a community of nations. These chapters reaffirm the primary importance of love in family life and related groups, but at the same time they present a more comprehensive view of the interaction of the family with the world and as a witness to the world. We are also urged to adopt a more positive attitude toward modern culture, a culture which encourages the development of persons and the society of persons. The other chapters are all marked by the same social awareness and personalistic emphasis.

Religion and life are fulfilled by each other. It is vital for us, therefore, to see clearly the intimate relationship between the two. Prayer is a total listening and responding to every way in which God manifests himself to us; life is watchfulness and responsibility: the same fundamental structures. The whole universe speaks to the believer; the heavens proclaim the glory of God. It is not only the firmament that speaks; even more, earthly things and man's ever-increasing knowledge speak. The new findings in the sciences that help us to a better understanding of man all proclaim God's glory and speak to us about his loving design for men. They appeal to us to be committed, to use and transform all these gifts into a personal expression of love and responsibility. Thus, the structural basis for our whole approach to life in the world is this love of God, the one Father of all, and gratitude for his wondrous gifts.

We have briefly noted Marx's error in making all other relationships—family, legal, cultural, moral, religious—secondary structures shaped by economics. Now we must make an examination of conscience: Have we not also slipped into a similar way of thinking about superstructures? For example, an outdated theology thought of conjugal love as secondary to fecundity, virtually a superstructure built on biology. According to the vision of the council, however, conjugal love is presented as the decisive reality, the source of genuine responsibility, generous human fecundity, and parental love. This is quite a different approach and leads to a loftier perspective of marriage as a vocation shaped by conjugal and parental love.

In this regard, we Catholics have not been the only sinners; there was also sinning among the separated brethren. A. Nygren is typical. His book *Eros and Agape* reflects a one-sided concern for "grace alone," and consequently for a purely supernatural understanding of redeemed love (*agape*). He keeps heavenly love high up in the sky, never allowing it to come down and join mere everyday human love. As a result, Eros, natural human love, remains miserably on an earthy level, divorced from divine love, whose "purity" and other-worldliness is ever exalted. Thus, God-given love, intended as a redeeming power in life, does not bridge religion and real life. It remains aloof, very akin to the Platonic ideas, while human love remains bedeviled because the path to God is a separate one and beyond man's reach.

This dichotomy has now been with us for a long time. It arose from a philosophy of abstraction which fragmented the human person and God's work in him. It put everything into separate compartments by themselves—grace, faith, love—although none of these things can exist by itself.

In earlier centuries, the Church had to preach the gospel of love for the benefit of the Hellenistic world, which did not have any genuine place for love in its system of virtues. Justice, prudence, fortitude, self-control were considered the four cardinal virtues, while love, the wellspring of them all, was omitted. Plato introduced *eros* as a striving for fulfillment in the highest ideas and ideals, but it remained outside the system of virtues. As a result, in some currents of Christian theology, man seemed to be constituted by these loveless virtues. Love was added only as a superstructure, or "super-nature." But what kind of a nature can the human person be said to have without genuine love; for is he not made in the image of God?

Confucius attaches primary importance to kindness and love which come closer to the understanding of nature and grace. In the "four holy books," he points out the gratuity of loving kindness and all the virtues following from it by saying, "The four most precious gifts which heaven has bestowed on men are kindness, gentleness, justice, wisdom."

When we speak about nature and grace, we praise God for bestowing on us his divine love in such a way and in such measure as no creature could ever expect. The gratuity of his love in redemption must always be emphasized, but never in terms of this dichotomy between a "pure," loveless nature and "pure" supernatural grace. My tentative solution suggests that we should rather insist on the sharp distinction between unredeemed love and redeemed love. On the one side, then, is the "un-nature" of unredeemed man who degrades himself, locks himself up in an I-centered personalism of self-fulfillment; on the other side is the redeemed man, living the Thou-We-centered personalism of human solidarity: a personalism of gratitude to God and dedication to his fellow men.

According to this view, instead of love being added to man as a kind of superstructure, the whole of man is granted a new perspective and is transformed according to God's original design. His wholeness is reinstituted. Then it becomes clear that the virtues of prudence, justice, fortitude, self-control are fully "natural" in God's design to the extent that they are inspired and guided by redeemed love. They are unnatural if practiced outside of God's design for man, in an I-centered way.

Man's nature is as God intended it to be: the nature of persons animated by unselfish love, who increasingly become mediators of his love and thus praise his name by expressing and fostering genuine love. So, instead of starting with a hypothetical "pure nature" (which we cannot define because we cannot know what it would have been), we must consider the whole matter in the perspective of the history of salvation.

MAN IN SOCIETY AND HISTORY

A genuine concept of natural law understands that man's nature requires a social and historical response. Man is always called to live in interdependence with his fellow men in this passover period betwen the past and the future, using the past to shape the "now" with a view to the future—the next moment, the next year, the future beyond this world. This is the existential aspect of man's nature, which is at the same time personalistic because it is finally the history of what goes on between God and man.

The Bible tells of this interaction of God and man: man is called by God to live in community; the community sustains its people in faith and hope; and God is present in all that transpires through the ages. Man looks for direction to Yahweh, the "One Who is There," who was with all the forefathers (whose heir man is), who is with those now confronted by the problems of our times, and who will be with the heirs of the future as shaped by man's present decisions.

Throughout the Bible there is a profound and pervading sense of community, of each individual's solidarity with "a people"; and the goal is to be a holy people. It is a way of thinking that we Christians must thoroughly recover if we are to develop, as we must, a much deeper understanding of the solidarity of salvation. Only then can we span the gap between religion and life. When we shall finally understand this, our social motivation will be genuine and our commitment will be made out of a sense of free responsibility.

The anthropology underlying the *Constitution on the Church in the Modern World* is greatly influenced by this biblical concept of man in history and in community. All aspects of man's life must be taken into account. Science, history, experience, all wisdom, along with the Scriptures, affirm that man is more than an isolated individual, more than a mere monad. In his biochemistry, psyche, spiritual yearning, and concrete situation in life, he is—and cannot escape being —a dependent and responsible member of a people, a "family" that now covers the earth. It is when he responds to this total reality that he establishes his wholeness and dignity as a man.

All this has to penetrate deeply into our natural-law thinking. Our present knowledge of the nature of man (still woefully incomplete but far more advanced than in previous centuries) makes incredible a "natural law" ethic based on a concept of man separated from the real world, from his fellow men, from the ongoing history of his varied interactions. We can no longer think of man's true nature, for instance, as denying him stewardship over certain areas of his biological nature. Whenever we speak of man's "nature," we mean man in his wholeness in genuine love. Until we learn to see him in his dependent and responsible vocation within the family of men, we are looking at him neither in the light of the Scriptures nor with the eyes of reason and human experience.

This perspective of the solidarity of salvation makes social commitment more urgent than ever today, when philosophies, decisions, and structures are already evolving which will eventually shape the organization of a totalized humanity. In his *Letters and Papers from Prison*, Dietrich Bonhoeffer asked the agonized question, "What protection is there against the dangers of organization? Man once more is faced with the problem of himself." And there was good reason for Bonhoeffer's agony. His own highly civilized country—once a "Christian" country—had already been organized for depersonalization and for death, the victim of decent people's noninvolvement in the shaping of public opinion and societal structures. They had not understood the oneness of salvation or the vulnerability of concern for self alone.

The *Constitution on the Church in the Modern World*, noting that "the progress of the human person and the advance of society itself hinge on each other," calls for a Christian personalism which is "always searching for better harmonization of personal, individual liberty and communal responsibility." The mission of the Christian in the world today should be essentially the fostering of this personalism on all levels and in all areas of human organization. Religion and life meet here. This accords with the nature of man, who is created in love and who knows himself to be constituted not as a person to manage or to be managed like a thing, but as a person to love and to be loved. The Christian task is to organize a world in which love is accorded the highest rank.

Is any other option feasible for the successful organization of a now-planetized humanity? Force, imposed management, separatism: all these things breed their own counterforces and eventual destruction. But love unites. In an I-Thou-We relationship, its energies combine and carry man-the-individual and mankind forward together with an ever-increasing maturity of consciousness and love toward the center and source of all consciousness and love, God, Creator of all.

Pierre Teilhard de Chardin, who so wonderfully combined the perspectives of paleontologist and personalist, poet and priest, envisioned all this. "Some day," he wrote, "after mastering the winds, the waves, the tides and gravity, we shall harness—for God—the energies of love. And then, for the second time in the history of the world, man will have discovered fire."

For this, *Oremus!*

8

INTERACTION OF PERSON
AND ENVIRONMENT

MODERN sociology has taught us how greatly the environment affects man's way of thinking and the whole pattern of his life.

By environment I mean not only our physical surroundings, the types of life and of individuals that happen to be around us; I also include the spirit of the community. In a broader sense, the idea includes culture, laws, public opinion, and the economy: everything that helps to shape the world around us and our relationships.

As individual persons, in our various roles and relationships, we are all partially conditioned by this total environment. An extreme theory asserts that man is wholly fashioned by his milieu. Marx held that economic forces produce the environment and the environment conditions the man. If that were true, no social personalism would be possible; man would be simply a commodity. Yet, to deny the shaping power of the environment and to say that man is free is too easy an

answer. Nietzsche's call for an Übermensch—a superman—
"who would transcend his milieu, resist the 'herd instinct,' and
strive to be solitary, a man beyond good and evil," was an un-
realistic call. Man is truly free, but if he makes no effort toward
shaping the social and economic structures and the public
opinion of his environment, then he is freely responsible for
any lack of progress, responsible for the fact that faulty struc-
tures and ideas harm personal relationships and gradually
destroy the dignity and freedom of many persons.

None of us can have any doubts—we have all seen it in our
lifetime—how powerfully man's thinking, his way of life, and
even the morality and faith of a whole people can be influenced
by environmental forces; but a true social personalism shows
us that man has the choice to be either a product or a con-
ditioner of his environment. The milieu unquestionably shapes
us to a great extent, but we are not captives of it unless we
abdicate our freedom to influence it. We can remarkably shape
the world around us if we make the effort and if we learn to
cooperate with other men of good will in this vital task to
which we all are called.

Modern findings about the influence of environment, and
especially about questions posed by Marxism, have had a
healthy effect on theology and on pastoral efforts in many
countries. We have learned that charity is not disincarnate;
love of neighbor is not a romantic I-Thou island without struc-
ture but includes true social awareness and an obligation to
create healthier cultural, economic, political, and social struc-
tures for our fellow men, as well as for ourselves. We realize
that individual conversion, to be totally valid, must include a
commitment to strive for a better, more fraternal community
and a more just world order.

Over the past twenty years, Germany has seen the develop-
ment of a new type of home mission and parish retreat, often
prepared for by serious sociological research into the problems
of the whole area. Some call it a "milieu mission," since it
focuses on the kingdom of God and its implications for a
commitment to the world around us. If the "save-your-own-
soul" style of mission is now out, conversion means not only a
new relationship to God and to fellow man but also a new

attitude toward the parish and the neighborhood, and beyond that to the larger segments of society.

A specific task of the Christian must be to develop small groups, genuine communities with respectful and dedicated personal and interpersonal relationships, and at the same time to have these groups commit themselves to society at large, even on an international scale. All this demands study of the interaction between family and environment, and study of the dynamics and interaction of the structures of parish, community, and other social groups and organizations. And finally, it involves a personal commitment to cooperate with other men for better structures throughout Church and society.

NEED OF FLEXIBLE STRUCTURES

A true social personalism combines responsibility for self and for the Thou with a commitment to promote better social patterns and the means of attaining them. We must have structures—there is no place for hostility to them as such—but they must be constantly tested as to their value in promoting the freedom and development of persons.

Professor Gustafson of Yale University, replying to a question raised at a lecture by a young woman theologian who did not see the need for continuity and structure in a personalistic style of life, called such a view "a new form of Roman Catholic romanticism." And he was right. This kind of romanticism dreams about a church of small communities and no structures. But even in a family, where we rely on each other, there must be some pattern and structured life, although it must of course allow for flexibility.

Recent efforts by some religious communities to function without superiors have not been very successful. There can be no doubt that we have to revise the old structures, but if nothing is organized, if there is no pilot in the jet, no rules in our life, the individual will suffer. Structures, however, should allow us to concentrate on those decisions which demand study and discussion of new approaches.

When reacting against the legalism and inflexibility of outdated structures, our aim must be not a structureless society but more humane patterns that will promote the welfare of persons and greater social harmony. Without some structure, we can have no community, not even a religious group of five or six brothers or sisters; for, without it, the community soon disintegrates. Even friendship, which does not need to be legislated, is based on a certain stability of behavior; if it is not, the friendship collapses. A family does not need a written code, but it does need a pattern whereby members of the family know the significance of their mutual relationships and what is expected of them. Of course, it must also be emphasized that society at large, characterized by a complex organization and structure of laws, is no longer humane if ample room is not left for the freedom of persons and intimate groups.

PERSON IN COMMUNITY AND SOCIETY

Social personalism, as I understand it, distinguishes the I-Thou relationships in the small group and community from organization, corporation, and society in a way similar to Toynbee's distinction between *Gemeinschaft* and *Gesellschaft*, community and society. Yet we must not separate into opposite camps the community of persons—the I-Thou-We—and organized society. Rather, they are complementary. We must see them as extensions of each other. In this light the primary importance of the freedom and responsibility of each individual person becomes apparent.

Social personalism is a practical working relationship based on absolute respect for each person and his fundamental human rights. Man is taken seriously in his wholeness: his body as the embodiment of love and justice, and his spirit—intuition, imagination, creativity—as the wellspring of cultural values. Social personalism takes into account the heritage of past ages insofar as it truly incarnates justice, love, and spirit. It shows us that the improvement of economic and social structures is not a mere matter of fate, does not come about automatically, but must be brought about in the conscious freedom of the individual and the community, with an acute awareness of the real possibilities.

Evidently this is an appeal especially for the elite, those who, according to the biblical expression, have received "five talents." One who claims to belong to the elite must be committed to the formation of a healthy world for the benefit of all; he cannot submit to being passively formed by society. What the task involves is not only an active expression of interest in social life; it is, above all, a love for the individual person, our neighbor, expressing itself by caring about a better community life and trying to attain it.

There are some people who have an extraordinary opportunity to shape community and society as well as themselves. Think of the saints or other great persons and their influence on history, the Church, and the world at large! But the real freedom of the person to shape the environment depends on his ability to collaborate, to gather around him a group of friends and thus to build up a community of right-minded people, or to inject himself into the most dynamic groups within a community. As responsible people they can then work for structures that protect the weak but do not stifle those who are capable of greater creativity and spontaneity.*

MUTUALITY OF INDIVIDUAL AND SOCIAL FREEDOM

Individual freedom will not survive if we do not make a common investment in it, by combining our individual energies and working for a better world. If it is true that in many ways the world molds us, it is equally true that our world is the result of the use or misuse of freedom by individuals and groups, and of failure by others to use their free initiative to shape it.

Social personalism emphasizes the effectiveness of freedom

* In the introduction to my book *Marriage in the Modern World*, I deal with this perspective of individual and social freedom.

through cooperation, but it also underlines the dignity of a man who dares to withstand the pressure of environmental forces when he is convinced that this is demanded by respect for a genuine scale of values and is the judgment of his own conscience. The great moments in life are those when a person refuses to conform passively to an errant crowd and enriches the world by a creative response to its needs. We must see this aspect especially against the background of a democratic cultural society.

Kinsey confuses the human community with a zoo (he was a zoologist) and equates the moral norm with a democratic majority. Since he found out, in his very imperfect study, that over 51 percent of American males at some time in their lives showed homosexual tendencies or related activities, he thinks that these "normal" persons, and not the 49 percent without such tendencies, should determine our judgment about homosexuality. How he got his 51 percent is a question in itself, but the publication of the results of his study influenced human behavior. The naïve believe in majorities, and since 51 percent were said to show this warped inclination, they thought they should follow, or at least consider as normal, a homosexual subculture.

When even intelligent college boys and girls are told that most of their peers have premarital sexual relations, they feel "abnormal" and come under pressure to conform to this majority pattern, or at least to brag of having done so. Just for this reason, such juveniles often indulge in sexual activity without feeling any real pleasure or self-fulfillment.

In view of the widespread immature desire to conform, it is of great importance to have men and women who dare to withstand the pattern of the majority. But such a person, who stands by his own convictions and expresses them frankly, must also realize that his actions will have practical results in the community only if, by his firmness and credible arguments, he can influence others to give corporate witness and commitment to the same convictions.

I am much indebted to the great personalists Ferdinand Ebner and Martin Buber, but I differ somewhat from their approach, at least in emphasis. They have developed, it seems to me, a rather one-sided I-Thou personalism and presented their philosophy about the I-Thou-We relationship almost exclusively in terms of marriage, the family, or intimate friendship.

We must greatly value, of course, such basic groups or relationships where we learn to have a respectful and warm relation with persons, but it is romanticism to confine personalism to this dimension. If all the other aspects of life are impersonal and are not imbued with a regard for persons, then even this I-Thou-We relationship will be disturbed and stifled by the massive forms of impersonal structures. Today's concern for better interracial relationships, especially for the social, economic, and civil integration of colored people, and the initiative displayed by responsible groups protesting war, or specific wars, or discrimination, are signs of a deeper understanding of personalism.

THE CHURCH AS COMMUNITY OF LOVE

In the past there was a certain tendency in ecclesiology to emphasize almost exclusively canon law and such concepts as jurisdiction and structure, thus alienating many personalists from the institutional Church, where it seemed that the institution was a goal in itself, an "establishment." The ecclesiology of the Second Vatican Council, however, attempts to strike a balance between the view of the Church as the mystical body of the Lord, the family of God, the fellowship of the Holy Spirit (all these are very personalistic expressions), and the Church organized according to various ministries, hierarchies, and laws needed for an efficient and effective working of the whole.

The theological perspective of the Church is that the people of God are gathered by the love of the Lord around him, united in "the fellowship of the Holy Spirit" (I Cor. 2:13-14). The Spirit guarantees the Church's unity.

This point had to be emphasized at the council because

some bishops forgot that we are united through the working of the Holy Spirit and our fidelity to him. They thought that Latin and centralization were the chief guarantees of unity, whereas they have been the causes of alienation and estrangement. Thus the Church had become, in many respects and in the eyes of many people, a rather stuffy body that put a damper on the spirit of spontaneity, instead of the "divine milieu" of love and faith which Christ intended it to be.

A decade ago, when Latin was still *de rigueur* in the Church, I wrote in an Italian book that I would like to advise the Italian Communist Party to show an excellent Russian movie in Italy once a week in the Russian language and make everybody attend it, with a view to promoting the unity of world communism on the basis of one language, Russian or Chinese. This would of course have been the most effective way to destroy communism!

The Church is a community of love, a structure of love and truth. Article 32 of *Lumen Gentium* (the *Constitution on the Church*) says, "By divine institution, holy church is structured and governed with a wonderful diversity"—not conformity or centralization, be it noted, which impoverishes life and interferes with witness. The whole Church is provided with a center in the Petrine office, with a view not to stifling other initiatives but to harmonizing them, to learning from them all, and to communicating effectively whatever good each represents.

One of the most striking expressions in this same Article 32 of *The Constitution on the Church* is: "In their diversity all bear witness to the admirable unity of the Body of Christ. This very diversity of graces, ministries and works gathers the children of God into one, because 'all these things are the work of one and the same Spirit' (I Cor. 12:11)." To learn more about social personalism in the Church, one should also read the Epistle to the Ephesians, chapter 4, and the first Epistle to the Corinthians, chapter 11. There is great insight to be gained, too, from an expression found in Oriental theology which says that the very diversity of grace in ministries and works gathers sons and daughters of God into one great family.

The point I want to make here is this: all this theology about the Church fulfills its role only when it is realistically reflected in the Church milieu—in the liturgy, in canon law, in the relationships between bishops, other officials, and the whole people of God.

At the first Pentecost, each person heard the Gospel in his own language. The great prophets foretold that in the messianic age all peoples would come and pool their riches together. The whole milieu of life in the Church should manifest this type of social personalism. This right self-understanding by the Church can greatly enrich secular society, which urgently needs a better form of organization, as well as greater appreciation of the spontaneity, generosity, and initiative of each person and each group.

A personalistic theology based on the Bible recognizes the importance of order and structure, of linking everything together in view of the unity of the Church of the Word Incarnate, but it does not place all its hopes on law and government. We need structures, but they must be kept flexible, ever open for the work of the Holy Spirit, all the more so in the present age of change. The great dangers connected with centralism, as we know from the past, should cause us to resolve to avoid all such things in the future without going to the opposite extreme.

In *Quadragesimo anno* Pius XI wrote that the principle of *subsidiarity* is the most fundamental principle of the Church's social doctrine. The principle means that a larger unit does not take over a task which a smaller unit can do equally well, but rather enables and encourages the smaller unit to fulfill its proper role. What a person can do must not be done by a group; what a small group can do must not be taken over by a larger one. The same is true of any organization. In government, what the township or the county can do should not be done by the state, and what can be accomplished at the national level should not be done by the United Nations. Whatever cannot be done by a smaller group becomes, according to subsidiarity, the responsibility of a larger group, but with a view to enriching the smaller group and enabling it to fulfill its own special role more effectively. Thus, the person will have an environment in which he can grow toward full maturity.

The question immediately arises: Does the Church have two

structures—one for the secular city and one for herself? Is subsidiarity for the secular city or empire only and centralization for her own organization? Pius XII replied emphatically that the principle of subsidiarity applies to the Church as well as to the secular city. Two conciliar documents, the *Constitution on the Church (Lumen Gentium)* and the *Constitution on the Church in the Modern World (Gaudium et Spes);* have drawn certain concrete conclusions from this thesis of Pius XII. I refer to the idea of collegiality, the increased role assigned to the laity, greater liturgical diversity, and so on—in other words, a flexibility of structures.

The great task today, however, is to bridge the gap between this deeper understanding and existing practice as determined by laws and administration, in order to overcome the tension between the concept of the Church as an institution and of the Church as a community of love. Institutions must be personalized, must be tested as to whether they are serving to enrich the person, protect his dignity, and foster harmony among all ranks of society.

Most important for the development of a healthy Church milieu is an attitude of openness toward divergent opinions within the Church herself. This is the only way Christians can improve the secular milieu—by means of a dialogue combining discernment and mature conviction. The Church's teachings must carry conviction, particularly with respect to the natural law. If Christians cannot distinguish between articles of faith and time-bound formulations, between a matter of faith and a matter of human tradition, they will not be able to give expression to views reflecting both wisdom and genuine freedom.

9

THE SACRAMENTS AS AN EXPRESSION OF PERSONALISM

THE first steps toward liturgical reform were taken by European youth groups after World War I. What they wanted was an experience of life and an encounter in the liturgy. Men like Romano Guardini and Pius Parsch gave them the rationale and a good deal of direction by offering them a theology of life, as well as by making the first real systematic effort at rethinking liturgical practice in a personalistic perspective. Other groups, like the French worker priests, even more courageously dared to try new forms of celebrating the eucharist which would give the participants the felt experience of being taken seriously as persons in a community of believers. The Second Vatican Council then achieved the first official breakthrough with its new understanding of the sacraments, and this, in turn, paved the way for the more personalistic outlook found in most of the other conciliar documents. A work on Christian personalism, therefore, cannot ignore the relevance of a personalistic understanding of the sacraments.

87

The liturgy occupies a key position in Catholic thought. If the faithful understand the liturgy rightly—as a concelebration of the sons and daughters of God for the praise of the one Father, the Redeemer, and the Spirit and Lifegiver—it will be easier to understand and shape the whole of Christian life as a concelebration of persons.

There is urgent need to reflect on this point today, because the clergy and laity who received their basic training more than ten years ago were imbued with a rather impersonal vocabulary and practice. Sacraments were spoken of as "sacred things," as "means" to be used, and so on, rather than as an experience of the presence and love of Christ. We cannot fully appreciate the meaning of the liturgical renewal until we understand this personalistic and existential approach toward the sacraments, which is both faithful to revelation and expressive of the spirit and language of our day.

The renewal has not yet achieved its full impact on the whole concept of life. The sacrament of penance especially, that great sign of peace and hope, is still not only being "administered" in a confessional box with a wall separating the priest from the penitent to whom he listens and speaks but also being hindered by a great deal of depersonalizing legalism and formalism. It is when we compare the older and newer approaches that we see more clearly the causes of tension in this and other areas. Much still has to be done before the sacraments become the personalizing events they are meant to be.

A SACRAMENTAL OUTLOOK TO THE WHOLE OF LIFE

A sacramental outlook can easily become impersonal and narrow, even mechanistic or magical, if we begin immediately with a technical exposition of the seven sacraments of the Church and the way they each are to be celebrated. It is important to see them first in a broader context, as an essential part of a whole sacramental economy of salvation with Christ as its center.

The word "sacrament" means a visible and effective sign conveying redemptive love. We must consider the whole created universe as a marvelous manifestation of God's glory and his love for the human person, for you and for me. God's creative word is more than just a mere word; it is both a message and a gift—it is *sacrament,* in short, involving the believer in a dialogue with God and with his brethren.

All the kindness, goodness, and respect manifested to us by our fellow men is a visible and often very effective sign that makes us understand better God's own love for us. Parents loving their children, spouses loving each other, neighbor loving neighbor—all are signs related to God's visible covenant of love with men. However, their "sacramental" quality comes through a growing awareness that God manifests himself in all these events, which in turn invite us to respond to him.

The Church itself is called a sacrament. "By her relationship with Christ, the Church is a kind of sacrament or sign of intimate union with God and of the unity with mankind" (Vatican II, *Lumen Gentium,* Article 1). The whole reality of the Church is meant to be a visible sign of salvation, of concern for men in the sight of God. There is no room for any magical concept or a clinging to outdated institutional forms.

The fullness of sacrament is Christ, the personal Word of the Father to us, the greatest and most visible sign of God's saving love for man.

In the sacraments of the Church we encounter Christ himself in community and learn, through grace, the three dimensions of love: we can love the heavenly Father only to the extent that we love our brethren, and can love our brethren truly only if, through faith, we are aware that Christ is in the midst of us. We honor the name of the Father only if we say *"Our* Father," remembering that we are brothers and sisters. For, without the "We" relationship with our fellow men, we cannot come to the full truth of the I-Thou relationship with God.

A sacramental outlook toward the whole of life and a right

understanding of the seven sacraments leaves no room for any form of a self-concerned individualism. In his *Imitation of Christ,* Thomas a Kempis says, "I was never less a man than when I was together with other men," meaning that he was not fully a person except when being undisturbed by others and alone with Jesus. We understand that this was his particular ascetical ideal, fostered by a monastic rule; but it is wrong to believe that this must be the way we are to understand human existence and the Christian vocation. There are some wonderful pages in his book, but we must remember the particular historical context: Thomas a Kempis made a vow to remain in his cell alone and therefore had a bad conscience when he was with other men. For that exceptional reason, and because of his individualistic training, he felt less a person when he was with others. Such a style of life cannot be the normal way of manifesting to the world the faith in the paschal mystery, which is the heart of a sacramental event. As I-Thou-We personalists, we meet our fellow men at every opportunity with a good conscience, knowing that we truly find ourselves when we seek others for their own good and thus meet Christ in them.

In the sacraments, Christ brings us, through faith and grace, into contact with the paschal mystery and teaches us his kind of personalism. The same love, the same spontaneous and faithful relationship Christ manifested to man during his lifetime and through the paschal mystery, he manifests here and now to you and me, in and through the community of the faithful in the sacraments of faith. Thus we are led out of the terrible desert of self-centered (Adamitic) individualism, which alienates us from our fellow men, into a Christlike personalism of brotherhood. We are brought to understand more existentially the doctrine of sin and redemption. We grow in awareness of the history of salvation and in our ability to take an active part in it, knowing that we cannot escape destructive solidarity with sin ("in Adam") unless we open ourselves to Christ's redeeming solidarity with all mankind.

A sacramental outlook to life commits us to the paschal mystery. We share in the life of Christ, and this means readiness to pay the cost of discipleship. Christ has redeemed us into his personalism by sacrifice, by his death, and the price of this discipleship is sacrifice. We are truly united in his sacrifice only when we put to death all egocentric concern. The struggle is between the "old man" in us and the new creation. Without this struggle, without denial of the selfish self, there is no hope that we will become new persons conformed to Christ. But this mortification will liberate, not stifle, our true self. It will do away with all those things that hinder the purification and growth of love, so that, in solidarity with Christ, we can join in his redemptive love for our brethren in the building up of his mystical body. We open ourselves to God and to others in a life of dialogue. This is the essence of sacramental spirituality.*

Christ continues to proclaim the Sermon on the Mount in his sacraments. In their very essence, they confront us with him as he teaches us the Beatitudes. (An outstanding biblical scholar, Joachim Jeremias, has an interesting theory about the Sermon on the Mount. He thinks it was a summary of Christ's teaching, a sort of post-baptismal catechism presented after the "sacraments of initiation"—baptism, confirmation, and eucharist—which adult catechumens received in a single celebration.)

All the lofty demands, praises, and promises of the Beatitudes are expressed in the sacraments, which, like separate voices in a sevenfold choir, proclaim the doctrine of Christ, the paschal mystery: the kingdom of God is for the humble, for those who know that they are poor; the kingdom of God is for those who are gentle; the kingdom of God, the knowledge of Christ and the heavenly Father, is reserved for those who have a pure heart, who think not of themselves but who open their hearts and minds to God and neighbor; the kingdom of God is for those who are willing to suffer, to be abused if love demands it, even to shed their blood for the glory of the one God and Father of all.

---

* This perspective is emphasized in the second volume of *The Law of Christ* and in the concluding chapters of my book *Sacramental Spirituality*.

In each of the sacraments, Christ comes into our life in order to transform it in accordance with that fraternal love which he showed throughout his life to the honor of his Father.

SONS AND DAUGHTERS OF GOD, BROTHERS AND SISTERS

When Jesus was baptized by John the Baptist, the heavens opened and the voice of the Father was heard: "You are my beloved Son" (Luke 3:22). Similarly, we receive, in baptism and through faith, the good news that tells us who we are: "Now you have become my son, my daughter. Immersed in Christ's love for all men, you are brothers and sisters."

This gladdening news should be celebrated with joyous songs and prayers by all who take part in the baptismal event, and particularly by the family, whose happy duty it is to communicate it to their child through the education and the kind of life they will provide for him. When God speaks and guarantees such a message of joy, the whole Christian community should rejoice, and from this event should flow a great reverence and respect for every person created in the image of God and reborn in the family of God.

In the sacrament of baptism, God takes the initiative, calling us by our own name, asking us to accept his redeeming love by responding throughout our whole lives. Through our promised response we are inserted in the people of God and given a share in the community of faith, hope, and love. It is adoption as son or daughter of God to the extent of our solidarity with the family of God, not outside of this solidarity. Our full adoption depends upon our being a loving and active member of his family. We celebrate our baptism not only in the liturgy —the community of faith, hope, and love with Christ—but wherever we show ourselves as true brothers and sisters in Christ.

The sacrament of baptism brings us to the reality of Christ's baptism in the Jordan, when he who had no sin wished to receive, among sinners, the baptism of penance which John preached. St. Luke notes that Jesus was baptized "during a general baptism of the people" (3:21). It was an impressive "Yes" to the burden it entailed: the reparation to be brought to God for all men. Christ speaks about his death as a baptism. "There is a baptism I must receive, and how great is my distress until it is fulfilled" (Luke 12:50). It is the way to manifest the full extent of his love for us.

If we say of baptism only that "sanctifying grace is infused," we fail to communicate the personalizing message and action. (Can we not find a better expression than "sanctifying grace" to communicate to men today this personalistic reflection of the triune life of God: our coming from him and returning to him, our "being-with" him and thus being consecrated, dedicated to our brethren?) The baptismal grace is a sanctifying presence of Christ's own gracious love, but the essence of this sanctifying action is that, through his love, we are given the wonderful knowledge of our new relationship to him and to his Father in heaven, and through him to our fellow men. We know, then, how to conduct our lives as sons or daughters of God. The love of God which we have received shows itself in fraternal love, and in this love we receive the full right of persons in the Church.

"I WILL GO TO MY FATHER"

Although we have rejoiced in the love of our Father and promised faithfulness to him at the time of our baptism, we are later very often unfaithful to some extent. If, in our weakness or even arrogance, we turn our backs on his love, sin against him, swear like Peter that we "do not know him," then Christ will come to us again in our shame and sorrow, so that we may experience his mercy and the marvels of his renewing action in his sacrament of reconciliation.

In the sacrament of penance, we are reconciled to God through reconciliation with the Church. The "blessed" sorrow arises not from self-concern because of a loss or fear of punishment; we grieve, rather, for the mystical body of Christ, knowing that if one member suffers, all members suffer. Our sorrow is filled with trust in God's mercy. Blessed is the poor man who, drawn by God's graciousness, decides, "I will go to my Father!" Thus he returns to the family of God.

An understanding of the sacrament of reconciliation makes us aware of the social aspect of sin: each sin makes us a source of contamination instead of a source of blessing and peace. We thus see that we cannot truly enjoy the Messianic peace unless we become instruments of peace, repairing the wrong we have inflicted upon the mystical body. Sacramental confession is not a magical purification; it bears fruit only if we are more sincere and ready to confess our sins to each other for mutual relationships in truth and sincerity.

The sacrament of penance was given to the Church when the risen Lord breathed upon the apostles and said, "Receive the Holy Spirit." Reconciliation means a new "spiritual" relationship. We are converted to the extent that we love our neighbors and humbly use all the gifts of God with a view to the reconciliation of all men. Through Christ, who has taken upon himself our burdens, we learn to bear the burdens of one another, to be forbearing and to forgive. This is genuine repentance and reparation, the only way to a rebirth of the person in Christ.

CALL TO MATURITY

The person who lives within the community of faith, hope, and love as a true member of the family of God gradually reaches a condition of readiness to assume full responsibility for his baptismal promises, as a person called to maturity. Once again, then, he encounters Christ in the sacrament which confirms him as his disciple. This is the sacrament of maturity.

The mature Christian has become fully aware of the liberating power of the love of Christ, the Messiah, the Anointed, who has consecrated himself for his brethren. He no longer lives for himself. Having gradually grown out of spiritual adolescence, he is conformed to Christ and is free in total dedication to his fellow men. "The law of the Spirit has liberated you from the law of sin and the snares of death" (Rom. 8:2). "If we live by the Spirit let us be led by the Spirit" (Gal. 5:25).

Christ, who was anointed by the Spirit to self-giving love, sends us the same Spirit so that, in greater awareness and greater maturity, we may live in solidarity with him, finding our true identity in him by bearing the burden of our brethren. The Spirit binds us together, and thus we come to know that search for self-perfection is not the focal point of our life. We cannot really possess and enjoy our capabilities and all the other gifts of God unless we use them for the common good. On this basis we test their value and urgency, and even renounce the cultivation of some of our endowments when the common good requires it. The gifts we have received from God will be charisms only to the extent that they are understood and used in the service of God's household.

"LORD, MAKE US ONE"

The center of all sacraments and the center of the Church is the eucharist, which is, above all, Christ with us personally, Christ in the midst of us, teaching us, as he taught the disciples gathered around him at the table of the Last Supper in the upper room. Always it is the event of the assembly of the faithful around Christ. The altar symbolizes Christ, who is the rallying call, reminding us, "I did not come to be served but to serve. I died for you; I have shed my blood for you." This is the height of true personalism—this greatest love that serves and lives, even dies, for others. "There is no greater love than this, that a man should lay down his life for his friends" (John 15:13).

In the eucharist, Christ reminds us that through his human nature all humanity is redeemed; in him the human nature is transfigured into purest love. We are brought together by the love expressed in his sacrifice, and shown that "in Him and through Him and with Him" all things can be transformed into expressions of this true love.

Very much depends upon a right understanding and celebration of the eucharist. We must rigidly exclude any impersonal or magical impression. We are truly celebrating the memory of the death and the resurrection of Christ if we believe in the liberating power of his sacrifice and therefore intend to sacrifice whatever hinders us from loving our fellow men. The eucharist is not some kind of sacrifice apart from love. We celebrate *that love* which drove Christ to rescue us from our egotism and unite us with him in redeeming love.

Some of the "old school" are rather violently opposed to the idea of concelebrating the eucharist. They insist that each individual mass is a sacrifice in itself. But, in so doing, they are forgetting the great message—that Christ's sacrifice unites and removes the obstacles to unity. Can we really share in Christ's sacrifice by maintaining a kind of "splendid isolation"? We must wholly abandon the thought that the mass can be celebrated without a commitment, first of all, to the love which is the source of all meaningful sacrifice. We need to become aware that each celebration of the eucharist should be seen as a visible pledge to oneness and solidarity: "That all may be perfected to oneness," since for this Christ has offered himself in sacrifice.

An ecumenical week was held recently in one of the outstanding abbeys of the United States, at which representatives from various Protestant churches joined with us in prayer and song while we Catholics concelebrated the eucharist. Once, as we came down from the altar, our Protestant friends noticed two Fathers celebrating mass by themselves in their stalls. Hitherto, our visitors had held the abbey in great esteem, but their esteem declined when they saw this. I later told the abbot of another monastery what had happened, and he said, "We have the same kind of priests here. We have to tolerate this sort of thing, but we try to hide it as much as possible."

We have here two understandings of personalism. One evaluates the sacrifice that was Christ's by isolating himself in order not to be disturbed by others. But Christ's sacrifice was to open his arms for all and to let himself be disturbed by the robber at his right and the braggart at his left.

I do not deny the value of a mass celebrated with only a server, if no other possibilities are available and provided there is openness or desire to be in community. But, since the mass is a visible sign of how Christ makes us one through sacrifice, I find it hard to understand the celebration of priests in absolute isolation, without even so much as a server, when they could so easily *concelebrate* the sacrifice of Christ and the oneness of the priestly people of God.

During the four war years I spent in Russia, I necessarily missed mass many days, owing to constant movement. But whenever we were where mass could be celebrated, I found some Russian house or a secluded spot somewhere; and invariably, in spite of the difficult conditions, there would be some good Russian people and soldiers who came to mass early in the morning. I did not have to celebrate the great sign of oneness without having any friend join me. But when I came to Rome in 1948, at my first mass a server started with me but left after the Confiteor. It was a solitary function. When this happened again, I asked the superior for permission to receive communion instead of celebrating mass. He asked why, and I said, "I would like to celebrate mass but not alone, not against the law to have at least a server." He answered, "You will have your server." Then we were always two; we were concelebrating our faith and our friendship.

Through the eucharist we enter—receiving and responding— into that sacrifice through which Christ wants to build up a community of faith and love. In so doing, we commit ourselves to all the sacrifices that may be necessary for us to advance our own community of love. We truly celebrate together Christ's priesthood, his sacrifice; and the mass becomes a community praising God if, through his gracious gift and appeal, we are becoming his family with one heart, one mind, and the ability to bear cheerfully with our different temperaments and opinions.

There was an interesting dispute at the council about this point. The preparatory liturgical commission drafted a very cautious text on concelebration, asserting, however, the right motive for it: concelebration is a fitting sign expressive of the oneness of the priesthood and the oneness of the people of God. The text was approved by the central preparatory commission. However, when the council Fathers received the draft, a quite different version of the motivation had replaced the original wording: if it is impossible to erect numerous altars, then, in extraordinary circumstances, the Church can *tolerate* concelebration. The change caused great dismay. Who had made it? Certainly not Pope John! There were loud protests, but no one was prepared to admit authorship. However, everything turned out happily in the end because the incident offered the council a good opportunity for insisting on the real motivation.

This motivation is very important for us. It is not just a question of an ecumenical gesture or a trivial new rule, as some imagine. Involved is a commitment to oneness on the part of those dedicated to Christ's priesthood and to oneness with the whole priestly people of God. Finally, now that the reforms have been enacted, priests and laymen can say together, "Lord, I am not worthy," and we all can eat from the one bread and drink from the same cup of salvation. If we are truly becoming one, this must be seen as a sign of Christ's nearness to his people. We cannot join him in the universal or the ministerial priesthood without this openness to each other, this unity signified by the one bread and the one chalice.

A CALLING THAT UNITES IN LOVE AND
SERVICE

We pursue our individual vocations as adults. Only in view of the covenant of love is it meaningful to speak of "vocation" in the sense of God's personal call which enables us to make a life response to him in openness to the love and the needs of our neighbor. We seek knowledge of this special call in prayer, in the natural qualities and capacities which God has given us, and in the circumstances and events of our lives. And whether this vocation calls us to a religious life or to work "in the world," to celibacy or to marriage, if it is accepted and lived in love, it is sacramental in quality throughout the whole of life. What counts is that a person is able to read the visible signs of God's loving design for him and respond in gratitude, not only in a liturgical, ritual way but in all the aspects of his whole life.

BROTHER AMONG BRETHREN

A man genuinely called to the priesthood is one who is touched by the love of Christ and his gospel to such an extent that the greatest privilege for him is to be able to bring the Gospel to as many people as possible. Like Abraham, he is ready to leave his family, his home, and his homeland to carry the Gospel wherever he is sent. Priesthood means being configurated with Christ, who is the servant of God and man, serving where the greatest need is. A priest is truly associated with Christ's priesthood if he is a humble and loving "brother among brethren."

In a study made by one of my students (H. Stenger, *Weisheit und Zeugnis,* Salzburg, 1960), several hundred young men were asked why they chose the priesthood. The results were impressive. They showed that the majority are motivated by concern for mankind. Joy of faith and love for their neighbors inspire them to serve the greatest need of their brethren. "There is need for good doctors, good lawyers, and so on" is a typical response, "but the best service we can bring to men is the proclamation of the joyous news, the message of the everlasting kingdom." Such ardor and such dedication surely make manifest the grace of the sacrament of holy orders.

The priestly vocation is essentially based on two elements: the joy of the Gospel, and the capacity to recognize in all human beings the image and likeness of God and to bring them to a greater awareness of this human dignity and their calling to manifest to each other God's own love. A priest is truly a man of God if he is a focal point of unity and charity.

Although *celibacy for the kingdom of God* is not a sacrament in the technical sense, it is a sacrament in a broader sense:

a sign of love and—to the extent that it becomes visible and credible as a witness—a sign of the kingdom of God present in the world.

The real value of celibacy and of a vocation to this state of life is to be measured according to the kind of personal relationships they produce. Celibacy for the kingdom of God means to be filled with the joy of God's saving and unifying love, which enables the person to rejoice in God and to dedicate himself to his fellow men beyond all bonds of flesh and blood.

Christ's own celibate life reveals the fullness of its meaning in the light of the paschal mystery. It is the life of the one who is anointed by the joy of the Spirit and sent by the Father to be every man's brother and Saviour. It is the power of his love, in which he consecrates himself, even to the death, as the greatest sign of a sacrificial love. Thus he redeems marriage and sex and all human relationships from the slavery of an egotistic individualism and a possessive, depersonalizing collectivism.

Celibacy is an offering which is meaningful only if the value of marriage is appreciated and the person is fully capable of married love, but, through the power and joy of the Holy Spirit, he or she becomes capable of living in generous dedication to God's people and to the Gospel. This life is lived in union with Christ's sacrifice and in a foreshadowing of the heavenly joy of the communion of saints.

CELEBRATION OF LOVE FOR BETTER AND FOR WORSE

Since marriage is the most intimate of all personal relationships, our understanding of the sacrament of marriage is a reflection of our understanding of personalism. Its constitution is reciprocal love. Marriage as an institution, the marriage legislation of Church and state, and the ethical norms for marriage must be tested according to this one great perspective: do they protect and foster the personalizing forces of marriage and the family; do they reveal discernment as to the true nature of conjugal love and the vocation of the spouses to convey the genuine experience of love to their children?

It is through the graciousness of the spouses to each other that God's grace in this sacrament becomes a visible reality. The healing and gladdening power of his gracious love for man, manifested in Christ, enables the spouses to accept each other as a gift of God and to help each other to become an ever more loving person, more capable of reciprocating a liberating love.

Self-concerned personalism causes the spouses to be ungracious, so that all mutual attraction ceases as soon as sexual relationships, and daily living, manifest a basic trend toward possessiveness, domination, and exploitation. But a true Christian personalist knows that the very essence of marriage is reciprocal love, a complementary relationship in mutual giving, cooperation in shared responsibility, a partnership forming the fundamental community of love.

In his letter to the Ephesians (chapter 5), St. Paul speaks of this relationship between husband and wife explicitly in the perspective of the paschal mystery. He teaches Christian women how to accept the humble social condition assigned them in the patriarchal culture of those times. That condition could not be changed at once and he could not know how much it would change in the future, but he realized that women have the same dignity as men before God and that a woman acts in full dignity when she loves freely, generously, and humbly according to her actual social condition. In this she follows Christ, who wanted to become all men's free and loving servant. And the husband is to be not domineering but cherishing, loving his wife as Christ loves his Church, with a love ready for any sacrifice.

True Christian marriage means not only mutual love, not only mutual giving, but also a grateful, joyous acceptance of love in this most intimate of personal relationships. Let me illustrate this by a very negative example. Sometimes the shadow shows where the light should be.

In Europe some years ago, a fine Catholic man came to me and said, "Perhaps, Father, you are the only one who can save my marriage. My wife reads some of your books and perhaps she will listen to you." Then he told me what had happened. They had seven children and for years had been a very happy couple. True friendship, mutual respect, and also great sexual harmony and joy had existed in their relationship. But then a friar had begun to tell the wife that self-denial meant that she should deny herself any enjoyment in sexual relations, and that she should suppress the pleasure involved in them and offer this as an atonement for priests who might be having trouble with celibacy. The husband explained that his wife had a very strong will and was able to obey this counseling, suppressing all pleasure and thus becoming unresponsive to all his expressions of tenderness. The conjugal act became for her a mere "duty."

I agreed to talk with her and found the case to be as she said. The woman said, "I will give him all his rights; he can have what he wishes." Her husband answered, "How could I wish that? I feel humbled, unaccepted; I do not want that kind of 'rights.' I did not marry the person you are now, one who renounces all joy. If my love is no source of joy for you now, you would do better to divorce me."

It took hours for me to explain to this poor woman how wrong she was, what a great insult it is not to enjoy the tender love of a husband, not to accept it gratefully. It is as wrong to reject the joy and pleasure arising from true love as to seek only the pleasure without a genuine love. There is no place in the truly Christian concept of marriage for the Manichaean tendency. God has created man and woman to his image and likeness (Gen. 1:27). Their relationships, including sexual union, should express the splendor of his love. According to God's design, the spouses should accept each other as the most precious gift of God (*cf.* Gen. 2:22-25).

A marriage is truly a success if the spouses experience what it means to be a person and to be loved with respect and dedication. Thus, they may realize, "If our love can give us such happiness, how blissful must God's love be!" Yet it is clear that even the best conjugal love cannot mean final fulfillment of the human person. Man is made for infinite love in the final covenant with God and all his saints. The humble and courageous acceptance, in mutual forbearance, of each other's human weaknesses and imperfections is part of the offering of love in marriage, and this too should lead to the one who alone is perfect, who is love and the source of all love and joy.

"LORD, HERE AM I"

Christ is with us again in our final hours in the sacrament of the sick, which brings us once again to the saving realm of the paschal mystery. This sacrament looks on sickness as one of the situations leading to salvation, not because of sickness in itself, but because of our faith in the gracious presence of Christ and the participation in his suffering and resurrection.

As for death, it can have two meanings. We can have the death of Adam, which means the final frustration of the vanity of a self-seeking life; or we can make it the greatest manifestation of love, trust, and faith, and the most important act of all, as was the sacrificial death of Christ. All those who, following baptism, have made the love, sacrifice, and glory of the paschal mystery the norm of their lives can render into the hands of God their lives now fulfilled and consummated, as an expression and witness of love for their fellow men and as the greatest possible praise of God. The grace and summons of this sacrament of the sick are accepted if the person who finds himself in this most decisive situation of life can respond with confidence, "Lord, here am I! Call me!"

10

THE KAIROS AND ITS
ETHICS

CARDINAL FAULHABER, a great churchman in the struggle against Hitler, adopted as the motto for his program *Vox temporis, Vox Dei*—the voice of our time is the voice of God.

Of course, he did not mean that the loudest voice or the prevalent opinion of the day was to be accepted as the voice of God. All too often it is the very voice of perverted power or opinion that manifests the evil to be resisted, even to the shedding of blood. What he meant was that one who listens will hear the voice of God and discern his will in the context of his own times.

In biblical language there are two different words for time. The Greek word *chronos* means time measurable in years, days, and minutes—a scientific measurement; the word *kairos*, on the other hand, can be translated as the present time of opportunity, the favorable hour, the time chosen by God which puts man to the test.

This concept of *kairos* is always fundamental to a truly Christian outlook. Today, in a new age, with our new knowledge, new problems, new options, and new visions, we find that more happens in one decade than happened in countless past centuries. It is therefore a vital part of a Christian existential attitude to be able to discern the message which the *kairos* brings.

As noted in an earlier chapter, Teilhard de Chardin was one of those prophetic voices who have helped us achieve the larger theological vision needed to understand the present times. He is optimistic with regard to the present and future because of his belief in an historical unfolding of the all-inclusive plan of God. In the *logos* of God all things are created and all things are directed back to him. He is the *omega* point of final fulfillment. Pope John too was a kind of prophet. He called his program one of *aggiornamento,* a word including *giorno,* which means "today." In his address to the non-Catholic observers at the Second Vatican Council, he said, with regard to his program for ecumenism, "Let each day bear its burden, use each day's grace." And no phrase occurred more often on his lips than "vigilance toward the signs of the times."

VIGILANCE AND PRUDENCE

The *Constitution on the Church in the Modern World* adopts the same perspective. The Church manifests herself as the true spouse of Christ by her vigilance to the signs of the times, the opportunities prepared by God for this hour. She acknowledges, however, that within her ranks there were—and are—"sleeping virgins," who do not see the hand of the living God writing in the social movements, scientific breakthroughs, philosophical and theological insights of their own times.

True vigilance involves prudence and wisdom. But we must understand how the Christian virtue of prudence, with regard to the hour of favor, differs from prudence in the humanistic sense. According to Greek and Roman philosophy, prudence is a virtue which helps man to see the circumstances and to understand how they can help him toward self-perfection, self-preservation, or to make correct civic decisions. He considers what is being proposed, the people with whom he is dealing, the means at his disposal, the mode of execution, and so on. The chief element here is man's power to foresee and plan, and the focal point is the self of the man who plans. Universal principles enter the picture because the man must preserve his consistency and the principles must harmonize with the special circumstances.

The Christian virtue of vigilant prudence transforms this humanistic concept. The most classical enunciation of the transformation is found in St. Augustine's *De Moribus Ecclesiae* (on the mores of the Catholic Church). According to his definition, "Prudence is love that is clear-sighted for that which helps it and that which harms it." The love, of course, is love of God, supreme good, supreme wisdom. We can therefore describe Christian prudence as the love which distinguishes between what helps and what hinders the way toward God. We have here a profound transformation of the I-centered or political understanding of prudence into an understanding that sees it as a mediation of love. Thus, prudence is the eye of love with respect to the present situation and its appeal or summons.

In the New Testament, more is said about wisdom as a gift of the Holy Spirit than is said about human prudence. In the biblical sense, wisdom includes the capacity of discernment in a man totally seized by love of God and of others, a man for whom the present opportunities—the *kairos*—are a direct summons from the God of history, who will bring all things to perfection.

IN THE LIGHT OF SALVATION HISTORY

To understand the *kairos*, we look to Christ, who enters into the history of man and transforms it. He manifests its dynamic direction and guarantees the final fulfillment. As man and as head of the human family, Christ accepts all that the Father has prepared for him. All the steps of his life are directed toward that hour on Calvary, followed by the hour of resurrection.

In the New Testament the *kairos* reaches its fullness in the incarnation, passion, death, resurrection, and final coming of Christ. These are the basic events which, in the perspective of the second coming of the Lord and final fulfillment, give meaning and norm of conduct to Christian life.

Christian ethics, then, is an interim ethics relating to this in-between time. The dynamic of the passion and resurrection of the Lord is found in each hour of grace and each decision. Judgment and salvation, which will be manifest in the final coming of the Lord, are already going on here and now. Thus, vigilance toward the present opportunities means preparation for the Parousia. Only those who are ready to recognize the Lord's coming in the here and now will be truly ready to greet him in his final coming.

That the *kairos* has come is the fundamental theme of all Christ's preaching. In Mark 1:14-15, Jesus comes proclaiming the good news from God, saying, "The time of favor is at hand, the kingdom of God is upon you. Be converted and believe the good news." The very heart of the Lord's teaching is this existentialist proclamation that the time of favor and decision has reached us here and now.

In an optimistic outlook toward present opportunities, we have a sign of discernment: those who preach the good news, the signs of our time, the time of favor and decision, like Pope John, are true followers of Christ, genuine believers. But those who are constantly fearful, who unceasingly lament the present times, are not true believers in the sense of history of salvation, although they call themselves Christians.

The question is whether we are going to believe that the Lord of history prepares for us a time of favor. In the Epistle to the Ephesians (5:14-16), St. Paul appeals to Christians, "Awake, sleeper, rise from the dead, and Christ will shine upon you." Then follows his fundamental appeal for a fulfilled Christian life: "Use the present opportunity to the full." It is true that he adds, "These are evil days," but from the context it is clear that this is meant for those who are sleeping or immobile, who do not care for good options at the present time. It is of the essence of Christian morality, therefore, to use to the fullest extent the present opportunities, the *kairos,* God's good time.

The hour of favor will not allow us to resort to *ifs* and *buts*: "If only my circumstances were different . . ." or "But I can't achieve my fulfillment here in this milieu . . ." How many members of religious communities, for instance, think, "I would be the happiest, most wonderful nun—or priest or brother—if only I were a member of a progressive community; I would work with such joy!" But since they are being put to the test in a conservative community, they should manifest Christ's endurance where they are and display hope based on faith in God's gracious presence. They can be the leaven that will gradually bring about the necessary changes. Of course, there are also those who err in the opposite direction, such as the nun who shocked me by saying of Pope John, "If this senile man had died some years earlier, all this trouble and turmoil would have been spared us."

The whole life style and self-excusing lamentations of these "if-and-but" people are the very opposite of a Christian existentialist's outlook. Men and women who are alert to the *kairos* will not yield to pessimism because of tensions. The growing pains in Church and society are signs of life which inspire hope, even when a few mistakes are made. Only the dead make no mistakes.

REDEEMING THE PRESENT MOMENT IN DISCERNMENT

The pastoral *Constitution on the Church in the Modern World,* Article 51, quotes the appeal in Ephesians (5:15) with the Latin phrase *redimere tempus.* This Latin translation has great depth: to redeem the *kairos,* to make available all the opportunities for redemption offered here and now. The literal translation from the Greek, "to purchase," has special significance too: to use this unique opportunity to purchase the best that is now available. Among Christians, as among housewives doing their shopping, one person chooses wisely and is enriched, while another misses the opportunities and remains impoverished.

Article 51 of the *Constitution on the Church in the Modern World* reminds us that, in order to "redeem the time," we must learn to discern what is the abiding core of truth and what is only cultural accretion from past times which may, and perhaps must, now be changed or discarded. Those who cannot discern these things will forever miss the good chances of this one present moment in history.*

The ethics of *kairos* is a response to God's loving design. At the center we find, not man who plans for self-perfection, but rather the person totally open to the whole perspective of God's plan. The history of the world, the history of man, the history of salvation, is, in its final meaning, a message from God, a word that reaches its climax in Christ. Christ, who is both messenger and message, is the humble servant whose ear God has opened to listen and whose eyes God has opened to observe the design of the Father. He is the "Yes" to the *kairos*.

PRAYERFULNESS IN RELATION TO THE COMING OF THE LORD

Kairos is an appeal from Person to person—from the loving God to a particular person and a particular community. The fundamental attitude of the Christian, therefore, is to listen, to observe, to be vigilant and open, and to act accordingly. This genuine openness and readiness are not possible without the spirit of prayer; therefore, Christ warns his

---

* This theme is more thoroughly developed in my book *The Christian Existentialist*, published by New York University Press and University of London Press, 1968. Here I only synthesize the personalistic and existentialistic perspective of an ethics based on the reality of the *kairos*, as contrasted with merely humanistic *prudentia*.

disciples, "Be on the alert, praying at each *kairos*" (Luke 21:36; *cf.* Mark 13:33). He does not tell them that they should pray twenty-four hours a day, repeating endless formulas, but that each hour, charged with unique possibilities or with particular dangers, should find them in the sight of God, trusting in him and alert for his calling.

For those who keep awake for the hour of favor, which is at the same time an hour of testing, the circumstances of daily life become a *kairos*. External events, along with the internal personal call, become one reality. The Holy Spirit, who renews the face of the earth, makes sensitive those who entrust themselves to him and are on the alert.

The vigilant disciple of Christ sees the external situation in a personalistic perspective. In events, God calls a person to greater sensitivity and responsibility toward neighbor and society. What the person receives from all the others in inter-communication and interaction is returned in gratitude to all the others through the best possible service in a concrete situation. The dialogue between God and man is *situated* and incarnate in the total reality of human circumstances. What makes the character of a person is openness in receiving and giving.

Thus the situation—the *kairos*—is not looked upon chiefly as an occasion for self-perfection but rather as a personal call for service and for receptivity to the dignity and needs of person. It is this alertness for the *kairos* that makes human life rich and fulfilled according to the degree of openness and dedication.

Each hour of decision tests our filial love for God and our fraternal love for each other. The vigilant person recognizes the coming of the Lord in his chance to serve the Gospel, to be witness for Christ's love for mankind. Looked upon in the perspective of the paschal mystery, it is the continuing coming of the Lord here and now to transform us through the calling of the Holy Spirit, to shape the history of man in accordance with God's intention. The wealth and density of the present situation becomes clearer to us in this view of the final coming of the Lord.

This is more than human planning. The final motive is not human self-perfection but the full manifestation of God's love and his glory and our response to it. The driving power is God's grace, his gracious and loving presence manifested in and through these persons, these particular circumstances and situations. He determines the hours and the opportunities. So the *kairos,* the hour of decision, has a splendor, an irrevocable, unique appeal.

RESPONSE, NOT SELFISH RECKONING

A Christian ethics based on the biblical concept of *kairos* comes to very different conclusions from those of some ascetical writers whose personalism is one of self-perfection and merit. Otto Zimmermann, in one of the most widely used textbooks of ascetical theology (*Lehrbuch der Aszetik,* Freiburg, 1932, p. 262 ff.), thinks that a particular occasion to do good does not oblige anyone, even if there is a special call through grace, since man can make a free choice to perfect himself and to earn merits by other means when he wishes. Here we have the same basic error as in Pelagianism. It is a self-centered personalism which, in the final analysis, depersonalizes man. An indication of the depersonalizing trend is the preference given to concepts like "goal" and "means to goals." Thus, the Other and the help granted him is subordinated as a means to one's own self-perfection. Such an outlook greatly diminishes alertness to the present needs and opportunities through which God, and not our own petty ego, speaks.

The ethics of the *kairos* uses a different vocabulary. Its whole approach, as so well expressed by St. Paul, is different. "You have received the grace of God. Do not let it go for nothing, for God's own words are, 'In the hour of my favor I gave help to you' " (II Cor. 6:1-2).

A right understanding of the *kairos* and of God's constant presence excludes inflexible planning and routine as well as inactivity. The *kairos* awakens man's spontaneity, initiative, generosity, without allowing any estrangement from life. It is an urgent and dynamic appeal for an existential response which man must leave behind him all reckoning and human tradition which would hinder him from being outgoing, alert, ready for the real possibilities and needs. It means a call to authenticity, uniqueness, to being one's own self with others on every occasion. Without undue tension or timidity, one can then grasp the opportunities that never will return in this same form.

EXISTENTIALIST CONTINUITY

Faithfulness to the *kairos* leads to a genuine continuity of life, since each hour of favor, with its challenging appeal, is a part of God's one creative and redemptive design.

The readiness to change and to grow according to the grace and appeal of the present moment is a renewed "Yes" to the everlasting covenant. It is trust in God, even if he leads us through a desert into an unknown future. It is gratitude with respect to the whole history of salvation and particularly our own heritage, which we can hand over to future generations —a new people—only insofar as we shape it and vitalize it anew. It is provident attention to the seed sown in our environment. All this is personalizing to the extent that we perceive the dimensions of salvation history and sense the urgent need for the solidarity of all mankind, which is so clearly a part of God's design.

In his fidelity to the call of the *kairos* the Christian personalist will not be overly anxious about his own identity. Yet, in his concern to be a faithful steward by making full use of all the potentialities presented by the *kairos,* his personal identity will shine forth to the same extent as his social consciousness. He consciously desires to use all his individual resources at this time and in this situation because he knows that if one person uses to the full the present opportunities, all persons, the whole community and the whole environment, are enriched, just as there is loss to all if one fails to respond to the vital needs and possibilities (*cf.* I Cor. 12:26).

THE SOCIAL DYNAMISM OF THE *KAIROS*

The *kairos,* while focusing attention on the uniqueness of persons and situations, has also a very strong social note. It calls not only the individual person to social responsibility; it is also an urgent appeal to communities to discern the signs of the time and act accordingly in solidarity, without, however, losing sight of the particular gifts and ministries of each individual. The whole community can be on the alert for God's design here and now only to the extent that the alertness and spontaneity of each person is encouraged and fostered.

Because of the realism and social aspects of the biblical notion of *kairos,* we are duty-bound to make the best possible use of modern research in social psychology, sociology, and other social sciences in order to gain a better understanding of all the complexities involved in human interaction. We can then discern better the limited but real possibilities open to us and make our contribution more effective.

It is true that modern sociology and psychology undermine many illusions about our freedom and what we can do, but they also point out real potentialities and opportunities—what we can best do according to our temperament and according to the whole social fabric of processes, relationships, and interactions. The proper use of these modern sciences allows us to plan the next steps, while it discourages all forms of routine and inflexible planning.

The Church, as well as the secular world, ought to use these tools in this age of change. We do not live in the Middle Ages, nor should we wish to return to them. Today is the day God has prepared for our generation and we must cope with our task with the tools and the thinking of today. But we need spiritual men to discern what the right spiritual approach is in this present hour of salvation.

THE *KAIROS* OF CONVERSION

The biblical concept of *kairos* includes a tremendous appeal to conversion. It demands a constant readiness to change where and when fidelity to the Lord of history demands it. This becomes more evident if we see each individual *kairos* in its essential relationship to the great *kairos*, the paschal mystery, which gives meaning and dynamism to all genuine changes in history.

Christ, who is truly the "Son of Man," opens new horizons, gives a new direction and value to the whole of history by taking on himself its burden of sins. He who was free from all sin offers atonement for all sinners. By entering fully into the suffering and tensions of human history, he reshapes it from within. Thus an event that seemed to be a curse for mankind is converted into the highest expression of fraternal love, to the glory of the heavenly Father.

The *kairos* means for us a humble acceptance of our past with all the consequences of our sins, in solidarity with mankind and all its yearning for redemption.

The ethics of the *kairos*, therefore, is one of continual conversion, not only of the individual but of all men, in the great perspective of the history of creation and redemption. For each of us and all of us, it must be an ethics of decision wherein man has continually to make a choice. The choice is between remaining attached to the Adamitic way of selfishness, isolation, arbitrariness, immobilism, and thereby being condemned to depersonalization—a mere number in a collectivism—or else adhering in fidelity to Christ's way, the way of accepting history and reshaping it, of being open to the hour prepared by God, of willingness to suffer for God and for fellow man.

11

SITUATION ETHICS: LEGALISTIC STYLE

Some modern existentialists advocate a form of situation ethics. Among the earliest exponents of such ideas were Eberhard Griesebach, a Protestant (his chief work is *Gegenwart, eine kritische Ethik,* Halle, 1928), and Ernst Michel, a Catholic layman, sociologist, and psychologist, who published several works on moral questions, including *The Partner of God* and *Renovation,* a book about marriage. In the English-speaking world, Joseph Fletcher is one of the best-known advocates of this form of ethics, and the trend is still going on.

But before going on to examine the views of these various modern situationists, we must recall the classical "situation ethics" condemned two thousand years ago by Christ: an ethics determined by legal situations and clinging to traditional formulas instead of manifesting the living God of the covenant. In Matthew 15:2-9 the Pharisees ask Christ, "Why do your disciples transgress the traditions of the ancients?" He responds, "Why do you transgress the law of God in the interest of your tradition . . . You have made God's law null and void out of respect for your traditions." He accuses them of "teaching as doctrine the precepts of men." In Mark 7:9 we find Christ saying, "How well do you set aside the commandment of God in order to maintain your own tradition."

The traditions of Moses and of the Jewish environment were partly expressions of the "order of love," partly responses to the signs of earlier times, and to some extent also imperfect expressions of the primitive knowledge available in those times. Originally some things were done because they were expressly commanded by God; but later on, as conditions changed, the rabbis taught many things that no longer related to man's vocation to follow the covenant of the living God. The Pharisees were addicted to a deplorable kind of casuistry and delighted in all kinds of petty applications and the advocacy of stereotyped principles. Thus they persisted in judging human conduct only in the light of their own legal situation, isolating it from the context of the essential law of God and from the situation of people in general.

We have an interesting example of this in the Dead Sea Scrolls. It was said that if a man falls into a pit on the Sabbath, even if the pit is filled with water, nobody should make a move to free him before the first evening star of the Sabbath arose. But the Lord rebuked this thinking. "But if a beast falls into the pit then you liberate him, and for man you do not!" The Pharisees were not seeing the central truth about the Sabbath: that it was meant not to restrict man but to benefit him that he might learn to adore God, the Father of all men in the community of men. They took the Sabbath out of context and judged the situation according to a fixed pattern, without thinking about the wishes of the Father of men. This is a typical example of the kind of estrangement induced by an unrestrained casuistry—the type of thinking which has tended to blight much of "establishment" thought down through the ages and against which the prophets fought so zealously.

The legalistic outlook focuses mechanically on the legal situation, considering only one abstract principle at a time and with absolute loyalty to this one point. It reflects an immature concern with the superficial rather than the substantial, with the words of the law rather than with the spirit.

TRUE SOURCES OF MORALITY

The legalist or formalist outlook does not distinguish between the different sources of morality—namely, man's innermost being and calling, the needs of persons in their growth toward greater maturity, their historical position and social adjustment, and the signs of the times. The legalist is concerned only with barren formulations, not life and persons. Having lost contact with man in real life, he has lost contact also with values and with the sources of life and truth. Bare principles, or rather formulas, guide him, and there is no consideration of how and why they were formulated or what human values originally justified those principles. For him, principles handed down by tradition and the authority of teachers need no justification in human experience; he does not see them within the whole framework of truth. In the final analysis, he has lost contact with the fact that God is the source of truth and has created man as a sharer of his love.

EPIKEIA: THE STRUGGLE BETWEEN SPIRIT AND LETTER

Aristotle made a major contribution in the human struggle against the constant threat of a legalistic "situation ethics." He insisted that every man-made law became brutal and unjust if applied in all cases without regard for various forms of life. He spoke of *epikeia* (*Nichomachean Ethics,* V, 4), the special virtue of prudence and of realism in the lawgiver. The lawgiver who is wise and prudent, he said, knows that no man-made law, regardless of the excellence of its formulation, can apply to all extraordinary situations. If he does not realize this and expects his laws to be mechanically applied in all cases, he is an unwise and imprudent man, unfit to make laws.

According to Aristotle, *epikeia* motivates right thinking about the lawgiver on the part of those who implement his laws. It is an insult to the lawgiver to think that his laws apply to every situation and to the same degree without exception. Moreover, the authority of the lawgiver can be eroded by a mechanical application of laws without respect for the social welfare. One of the most beautiful treatises in the theological Summa of St. Thomas Aquinas is the one on *epikeia* (*Summa theologica*, IIa, IIae, 120). He holds with Aristotle that it is vicious to apply human laws mechanically, without respect for the dignity of man and the common welfare.

St. Alphonsus Liguori poses the question whether *epikeia* applies only to man-made laws or to the formulations of the natural law as well. Surprisingly, he says that it applies also to formulations of the natural law. Alphonsus is convinced that in extraordinary situations a decision which contradicts a formulation of a natural-law principle can be justified if there is enough evidence that the action is free from malice (*Theologia moralis*, I, 201). The question becomes actual in vital conflicts of duties. If we interpret strictly the declaration of the Holy Office of February 2, 1956, condemning situation ethics, then St. Alphonsus seems to be condemned, although Pius XII has declared him the patron of confessors and moral theologians.

My personal opinion is that *epikeia* does not apply to what is truly natural law. But if one understands "natural law" as a collection of principles formulated in another age, which can never fully express man's calling at the present time and under all circumstances, then it does apply.

One of the most striking examples of this type of situation ethics, which attaches greater importance to the needs of persons in growth than to abstract formulations, is the famous case concerning interrupted intercourse, which St. Alphonsus deals with twice in his *Moral Theology*. Along with almost all other moralists of his day, he taught that it was contrary to natural law for the husband to spill his seed outside of the woman. But he said it was "not so absolutely against natural law and intrinsically evil that it would not be justified in some situations" (*Theologia moralis*, VI, 918). (Incidentally, one of his questions reveals him as one of the first moralists who suspected that woman also contributes something to conception—*ovule*, but he called it "sperm of the woman.") So he first teaches that interrupted intercourse is against natural law but then says that "if there is a *just cause*," it may licitly be interrupted, even though, "through the excitation of nature, orgasm will follow."

Sanchez, a famous Jesuit moralist, had already declared, in his work on matrimony, that to interrupt intercourse is against natural law, but that for a very grave reason, "*gravissima causa*" —for instance, if during intercourse the coming of a foe would threaten the life of the spouses—it would be lawful to interrupt the act. So what is called a formulation of natural law is not absolute in the sense that it requires a mechanical application under all circumstances. A discussion follows as to whether *epikeia* can apply only to the "most serious" causes, as Sanchez was teaching, or if an exception might also be made for a grave reason, such as if children should approach at the time. St. Alphonsus decides in favor of *justa causa*, or a good reason such as danger to the woman's health (*Theologia moralis*, VI, 945).

Theologians today approach the question from a different angle. We ask whether we can formulate all the principles of the natural law for all times and all circumstances. Our outlook with regard to man's nature and the natural law includes the historicity of man: man being called as a person, but a person called at this particular time and according to this particular human situation.

It is remarkable that even in the age of absolutism there were moral theologians like St. Alphonsus Liguori who taught quite clearly that *epikeia* could be applied to all man-made laws and even to secondary formulations of the natural law. But, unfortunately, those Church leaders who are not theologians but are chiefly administrators concerned ever about external order and organization do not believe in *epikeia*. They would not be inclined to agree with Aristotle that it is an insult to the lawgiver and those in authority to think that man-made laws and precepts can be applied mechanically. One of the chief reasons for the present authority crisis in the Church, and why there are so many protests, is that some in authority would like to impose a quasi-mechanical application of Church laws.

SECURITY COMPLEX: FEAR OF DISCERNMENT

During the spring of 1967 I was speaking to a bishop who said that we moralists ought to be very severe with people about the application of the law. For instance, prior to June 29 of that year, no priest was allowed to make the slightest change in those things which, on the twenty-ninth, would be changed by law. The bishop's chief reason was that, if any exceptions in the law were approved or tolerated, priests would go even so far as to discuss celibacy and other important laws of the Church! Another bishop even threatened to suspend any priest who anticipated by one day before the legal date the slightest change ordered by Rome.

These are classical cases of the desire to be safe: there must be no questioning of laws. Such bishops do not realize that everything will be challenged if we make everything absolute, while otherwise only a small part will be challenged. But if we learn to look for the justification, meaning, and value of every law, and try to see how it is related to God, his commandment of love, and the signs of the times, then we will achieve that mature attitude that never sets aside the commandments of God in order to preserve human traditions and precepts.

With regard to celibacy, for instance, I am absolutely convinced of its great value if freely chosen and joyously observed for the kingdom of God, and of the necessity for fidelity by those who have freely and responsibly chosen it. But I feel that the law on celibacy is one of the cases where we cannot set aside the commandments of God in order to maintain human traditions. If there are not enough authentic vocations for the celibate life, for example in Latin America, then the Church has a duty to provide people with good priests by ordaining mature married men.

If the present legislation causes more scandals than another solution, why should serious thought not be given to making changes for the common good? The Church has tried, and is still trying, to resolve the extremely serious situation in Latin America by sending thousands of foreign priests there. This effort deserves praise and admiration: celibacy enabled these priests to help build up the Church in other countries. But the freedom of the Church to seek other solutions, if necessary, must not be hampered by any law she has imposed on herself in other times and under other circumstances. While we must affirm the value of celibacy, there can be discussion about the proper legislation.

The Church has to love celibacy for the kingdom of heaven as much as Christ did, not more and not less. When he gave the Church apostles, he chose married men as well as unmarried ones, since men rarely lived in celibacy at that time. We can pray, we must pray, for more vocations to celibacy—this is an important witness. But the Church is simply not allowed to say, "We have made this law and therefore we can disregard any other law, as, for instance, the need to ordain priests to celebrate the Eucharist with the people."

ABSOLUTES IN ETHICS

Almost everyone agrees today that during past centuries and decades Catholic manuals of moral theology maintained too many "absolutes," especially with regard to liturgical matters. An example is the teaching that under no circumstances whatsoever could the eucharist be celebrated without using an altar stone consecrated by a bishop. They even went so far as to prohibit, in a very apodictic and absolute way, priests of the Latin rite from celebrating mass on an altar of an Eastern Catholic Church, where, instead of an altar stone containing the relics, an "antimension" (a linen containing relics) is used.

Today it seems ridiculous that intelligent and open-minded men had to go through a crisis of conscience and obedience until they realized that such things cannot be absolutes. In June 1941, a few weeks before the beginning of Germany's war with Russia, I was in the medical corps stationed along the Russian frontier. I was joined by four other young priests. I told them that, in spite of the law of the Hitler regime forbidding all religious activity, there were possibilities to offer the eucharist for believers in the army. These four men all were generous enough to risk being jailed for such illegal activity. But when they discovered that they would have to celebrate either without an altar stone or on the antimension of the Eastern Church, there was real trouble. Finally, I told one of them that I would take on myself all "mortal sins" on behalf of sacred stones and vestments in order to keep him free from sinning against the Lord's injunction, "Do this in memory of me," and against so many other aspects of the Christian faith, if he would only not deprive hundreds of men of the eucharist just because of the lack of an altar stone.

LEGALISTIC SITUATION ETHICS IN ADMINISTRATION

Young priests were not the only ones to be troubled by this erroneous teaching about too many absolutes. "Situation ethics" of the legalistic type enjoyed many a triumph in chancery offices, although not because of lack of good will. One example will illustrate thousands of such legal cases.

In 1950, during a home mission in a West German diocese, a couple came to the missionaries to explain their case. Forty years before, the husband had married a girl who did not know the meaning of marriage and refused intercourse. The priest whom the man consulted at that time told him that his marriage could be annulled, and the man obtained a civil divorce. Actually, however, he never got the annulment, although he went through a series of frustrating procedures. Finally he married, civilly, another Catholic girl. Since he had

left his home town, the ecclesiastical invalidity of their mar-
riage was not known to anyone, and consequently not known
in the parish where they approached the mission priest. They
could assure him that for the past fifteen years they had lived
"as brother and sister," without any sexual intercourse. They
had gone to mass and said the rosary together almost daily.
But they had never received absolution, never received com-
munion; and now they asked if they could finally be admitted
to communion, at least during the mission.

The diocesan office had reserved the case, and the mission-
aries, not realizing that canon law provided them with faculties
in certain cases during home missions, applied to the diocese.
The response was: "Since by our orders issued in 1941 we are
bound to grant such requests only if both persons have passed
their sixtieth year, and since this wife is only 59 years old now,
we are unable to grant the request. They cannot receive the
sacraments." They had bound themselves to a law and nothing
else mattered! The basic reason for such a law could only be
to prevent scandal. It could easily be assumed that a couple
about the age of sixty were living as brother and sister. But
in this case, by keeping the "law," they provoked scandal,
since people now would wonder why they had not received
holy communion during the parochial mission. So the words
of God were disregarded, "Whoever comes to Me, I will not
cast him away." Instead of looking into the meaning of their
own law and the special situation and needs of the persons in-
volved, as well as the common good of the Church, these
diocesan officials transgressed the most fundamental laws of
God because of their mechanical application of a rule.

This legalistic attitude is, of course, not confined to the
Church, although we must recognize that it is worse if done
in the name of the Church, in the name of those, that is,
who are consecrated in the highest way and anointed by the
Holy Spirit.

We need to examine our consciences on this point and ask
ourselves whether we are sometimes attempting to avoid greater
sacrifices or greater generosity by protecting ourselves behind
some man-made law and applying it mechanically. The whole

matter of absolutes and the absolute application of laws has to be restudied in a personalistic frame of thought. The decisive criterion must be the scale of values: the person's goodwill to grow in faith and love, the good of persons, and their growing capacity to reciprocate love.

12

SITUATION ETHICS
TODAY

Moralists at both extremes of the situation-ethics pole should agree on a solid definition of morality as "fidelity to the human vocation to love." Authentic theologians have always taught that love is man's highest vocation and that man will be judged according to his fulfillment of this great calling. But, in the practical application of this norm, the two groups—the rigid legalists and the all-out situationists —disagree sharply. "Observe the law; that is love," says one, while the other says, "Observe no law except love."

To focus on a supposed conflict between love and law is to miss the fundamental contradiction. Between love and law, as such, there is no incompatibility. Law protects love and conveys a concept of love. Properly formulated, interpreted, and administered, law defines and guards the outer boundaries of the order of love, beyond which lie arbitrariness, injustice, and self-serving utilitarianism: these are the real incompatibles. The contradiction, then, is not between love and law but between the true countenance of love and those attitudes which can never fit into love's essential character. What is needed is a long and searching look into the face of love, as well as a searching attitude with respect to the real meaning of law.

THE COUNTENANCE OF LOVE

In a certain sense, it can be said that love is the only absolute value and nothing apart from it is an absolute value or law. But then we must know what we mean by "apart from." We cannot mean that sincerity, gentleness, temperance, justice, the courage to sacrifice, or respect for self and others are something apart from love. They are the very features of the countenance of love, the elements of its composition. In them and through them, love shows its face. Love is all of morality, not in the sense of excluding the other virtues but in the sense of including them all and giving them their real meaning and value.

In the Bible, love has a definite physiognomy. It is "never boastful nor conceited nor rude, never selfish, not quick to take offence. Love keeps no score of wrongs, does not gloat over other men's sins but delights in the truth" (I Cor. 13:4-7).

The thesis of extreme situationists asserts that there is no prohibitory principle that always binds, and that everything except love is relative, changeable, and open to varied interpretations. In the final analysis, this means that love is a "sphinx," something that looks at once like a human, a lion, a winged creature—an inscrutable thing without a countenance. It could be at the same time agapaic and unselfish, and also utilitarian and pragmatic. Or it could fall from the sky as atom bombs on Hiroshima and Nagasaki. In Joseph Fletcher's book *Situation Ethics* (Westminster Press), there are a dozen mutually exclusive definitions of love.

In a debate at Yale University, I asked Mr. Fletcher if the principles which he said must be transgressed if love so demands included, for instance, that which forbids rape as immoral and criminal. Were there situations where rape is good in itself and not wrong in conscience but only a crime against law? He replied, "Of course"; since there is no unbreakable principle, why should rape not be justified sometimes by loving concern! Had he really looked into the countenance of love before he made that answer? Or is love, to him, a sphinx? Or did he have a clear concept of what he meant by rape?

Legalists, too, have failed to see clearly love's countenance, since they do not look to persons and personal relationships where love discloses itself. They are concerned not with the unique person-who-acts but with the act in abstraction. As a consequence, their all too materially worded rules or norms result in fixed, mechanistic applications that do not respect the variety and development manifested in God's creative design. They do not consider essential differences, do not see the existential person, or man in growth, or humanity in growth. They draw a very strict boundary line—which is necessarily a minimalism—and apply it alike to all circumstances, all levels of age, talent, and varieties of society. Sin is analyzed apart from person, and some even profess to know the precise point at which sin ceases to be venial and becomes mortal.

How interesting, this difference between mortal and venial sin! When I published my book *The Law of Christ,* one of these legalistic moralists said to me, "Father Häring, I cannot accept the basic approach of your moral theology. For me the main objective of scientific moral theology should be to determine with geometric accuracy what God takes seriously and what he takes less seriously." For him the whole problem was to determine the boundary limits once and for all. His attention was so wrapped in the prohibitory laws that he no longer saw the dynamism of the human vocation that calls for an ever more perfect understanding and fulfillment of love.

Once it has revealed itself in reality, once it is clearly discerned, one knows that love is the authentic expression of the meaning of persons and human relationships. But the ethics of the signs of discernment have not yet been sufficiently developed with regard to the matter of love, law, and situation.

For a theistic and personalistic ethics, it is evident that no law can be absolute or valid if its application here and now contradicts the exigencies of true love. Every moral principle must justify itself in its capacity to express the basic reality of love and promote it. But this ethics starts not with love as one law among others—even though the most compelling one —but as a revelation of the encompassing love of God himself, who wishes men to concelebrate his own love.

In this perspective, love is seen as the constitution of man and his destiny, and the ethics that develop from this are not material laws or principles but the living expressions of love. There is no imposed commandment to love; yet there is surely an absolutely obliging call to love, in the sense of the demand of man's innermost being. As the supreme expression of the whole person in community and before God, love makes clear the exigencies of personal dignity and of life in a community of free persons.

THE ORDER OF LOVE

To a certain extent, all morality is situational in that it involves the individual response of a particular person in a particular situation to the personal call of God. But there are essential characters of love, and the moral demand—the law— is that each person make a serious and constant effort toward a better understanding of love and its mediations. In this understanding, we find numerous criteria necessary for discernment.

The biblical moral message is not centered on laws apart from love. The Sermon on the Mount and the Farewell Discourses of Christ proclaim the blissful and compelling power of God's love and man's happy capacity to respond. What the biblical message gives to the mature Christian is the ability to discern between true love and its counterfeits, between the rich harvest of the spirit and the bitter harvest of the selfish nature (*sarx*). The fruits of unselfish love, awakened by the Holy Spirit, are joy, peace, patience, and the rest, and "there is no law dealing with such things as these" (Gal. 5:22-23). But the fruits of selfishness—those things that are outside the order of love—are judged "under the law."

If, therefore, we are to deal adequately with the morality

of a great variety of persons in a great variety of circumstances, we must watch for signs of discernment, ever searching and interpreting anew what is abiding and what is changing in the formulations, with a view to other times, other persons, other circumstances. This is the way toward a Christian "situation ethics" which, however, always remains within the order of love, justice, temperance, and so on. There can be no mechanistic answers, no careless definitions, no misunderstandings of what love is, because love itself calls for an ever better understanding of its demands and, therefore, of what the law really is in view of those demands. Love does not tolerate arbitrary choices of lower values against higher values, either because "there is no law that binds" or because "there is a law which says . . ." Love controls law as well as our choices.

A MATTER OF INTERPRETATION AND VOCABULARY

Not infrequently, situationists attack "law" when what is at fault is not the law but the *vocabulary,* the interpretation, or even their own lack of perception. In a public debate, Mr. Fletcher brought up the principle "Thou shalt not lie," and recited a favorite example of the difference between "lying Baptists" who, by reasonable lies, want to preserve others from great trouble or danger, and "non-lying Baptists" who assert that truth must always be spoken, no matter what may happen to others. Mr. Fletcher, who is Anglican, said, "I belong to the lying Baptists."

My response was, "I make no such choice. My choice is whether I belong to the intelligent or unintelligent Catholics." And I gave the example of some nuns who in Germany during World War II were taking care of many unfortunate children. Under Hitler's orders, the SS came to the orphanage and asked, "How many children do you have who are afflicted by this or that kind of disease or are mentally retarded?" In a few cases, the nuns—in great distress but with literal "truth"—answered the spoken question, and the unfortunate children were taken off to the gas chambers. Other nuns answered simply, "We have no such children," and that was the truthful answer to the question that had really been asked, because they had no children whom they would send to the gas chambers. Out of an intelligent sense of responsibility, these nuns did what is easily explained by anyone familiar with the philosophy of communication. They realized that not only the words but also the context can change the substance of a communication. They interpreted the context of the presence of SS men, their intention, and the political climate of the times, and rightly answered what had actually been asked.

So language must be studied. What is it? It is a communication between persons. Here the SS men did not want genuine dialogue but cooperation with their wicked design. The only real truth could be a firm and practical response of resistance to the evil they had in mind.

If we talk about the morality of an action, we cannot simply label it with a name picked from the dictionary and make a decision on the basis of that name, but we must look to the moral meaning of this particular action according to its motivation and full context.

A few years ago, a reader of my column in the Italian publication *Famiglia Cristiana* asked the following question: a captured spy, serving a country whose freedom is greatly threatened, is in possession of secrets which he knows brain washing could make him betray, and this betrayal would endanger peace on earth. May this man take his own life in this case? May he "commit suicide"?

My response began with the general principle of Catholic moral theology: suicide is immoral. If one is sure that this is suicide in the moral sense, with its characteristic malice, then there is no doubt about its immorality. But the real question is: should it be called suicide at all? How do we define suicide? There are all kinds of cases where people have disposed of their lives. Christ himself said, "Nobody takes away my life, I give it myself," and he gave it in the greatest offering of love. That was the supreme sacrifice, not suicide.

At the other end of the scale is the type of suicide seen in Dostoevsky's *Brothers Karamazov,* which was rebellion against

God and was intended to show that "I am the Lord of my life." In many other cases, suicide is meant to show that "my life is without any value," which is a form of desperation. Between the two extremes, there are all degrees of loyalty and lack of loyalty to principles, psychological impulses, cowardice, unconscious rebellion, or despair.

A confrere once told me about a decision he had made when in a concentration camp in Czechoslovakia. He had worked for the apostolic delegate and knew things that should not be revealed. He was put under extraordinary stress—without food and under the heat and glare of horrible lights—and subjected to long, exhausting hearings. He said to me, "I was sure that the next time I would break down, being at the end of my strength, and would betray everything. I knew my psychological forces were exhausted." So he decided to make an unreasonable attempt to escape. The chances were ninety-nine to one that he would lose his life by the method he chose.

Against all odds, this priest did reach safety, barely alive. But the question is: what is suicide? Did Socrates commit suicide when he drank the hemlock, as he was condemned to do by unjust judges? If he had not, he would have been strangled. Did the Japanese nobleman commit suicide in the eyes of his countrymen when he resorted to hara-kiri on being ordered to do so? Goering took poison two hours before he was to be hanged. What was the moral meaning of this act? Jan Pallach loved his life, mother, and bride. By the sacrifice of his life, he gave testimony that fear cannot break the desire for freedom of those to whom bodily life is not the highest value. Did he commit suicide in the moral sense of the word?

No two cases are alike in all respects. What is just a word in the dictionary may be, in one case, a most generous response to the needs of one's fellow men, understood and meant as a loving response to God's call, and in another case it may be a defiant rejection of his holy love.

The matter of abortion brings us to another delicate area where errors about value-judgments are not uncommon. The word itself relates to a physical reality. To simplify moral distinctions, however, moralists have distinguished between "direct" abortion, which is not allowed, and "indirect" abortion, which may be justified. A famous Austrian gynecologist published an account of the following case.

He was faced with the problem of extremely dangerous bleeding in the womb of a pregnant woman. No ordinary means could staunch the bleeding and there were only a few minutes in which to save the woman's life. He decided to take out the embryo and compress the womb. Compression saved her life and even her fertility, and later she had several healthy children. The doctor related the case to a famous moralist who replied, "You should have taken out the whole uterus and then it would have been an indirect excision and therefore indirect abortion. But now, by taking out the embryo, you have committed direct abortion." Here we have a typical case of a bare material definition by a legalist who does not look to values and meaning. "Direct abortion," "indirect abortion": what a morbid game with words!

My approach to the same problem is that it is an abortion in the medical sense but not in the moral sense. (In most countries this would not be considered an "abortion" even in the legal sense, but I want to emphasize the difference between the moral sense and the question of legal sanctions.) In the moral sense, abortion occurs when a person decides to destroy the life of the embryo or fetus. Here the doctor did not make a decision to deprive the child of the right to live; it was already deprived of this right by circumstances. He acted as interpreter of the real situation, interpreter of divine providence, and he saw that although the fetus had no chance to live he might still save the life of the mother. If he did not attempt to do so, he would be depriving the mother of the right to life. His decision was not abortion in the moral sense. He even saved the mother's fertility—and the persons she later conceived—which the legalist's method would have sacrificed in order to save his "principles."

So we must be cautious about obedience to mere words when we deal with moral problems. Our obedience must always be to the real meaning, the enduring values of human acts within the reality of actual situations.

DISTINCTION BETWEEN MAN-MADE LAW AND INBORN "LAW"

It is part of the common tradition of Western culture that no man-made law (positive or statutory law) can oblige under all circumstances. Neither legislator nor administrator can include cases where literal obedience to the law would be meaningless or harmful for the common good or a burden out of proportion to the goal of the law. Aquinas held that "to cling to the letter of the law when this is not fitting is wicked. Therefore the code of laws says that doubtless one sins against the law when one clings to the words and thereby acts contrary to the intention of the legislator" (*Summa theologica* IIa, IIae, 120 ad 1).

But there is a vast difference between positive laws and those moral norms which are expressive of the innermost being and calling of the human person and therefore of God's loving intent for man. And it is chiefly because of the failure to make this clear distinction that rigid legalists, as well as modern situationists, most frequently quarrel about the primacy of "love" or "law."

How frequently extremists at opposite poles resemble reverse prints of the same picture! The typical legalist is in many cases a stubborn situationist. He has a legal situation which does not fit into the order of love, yet he clings to the demand of the "legal situation" and forgets about God's law of love and the true needs of persons. On the other hand, the situationist has a situation of "love" which may be utilitarian rather than agapaic, or individualistic rather than communal; and he acts, in the name of loving intention, at the expense of the higher demands of the human calling expressed in genuine moral norms.

Both approaches seduce one to mediocrity. One whose attention is riveted on rules and abstract principles will never lift his eyes to the heights for criteria: to God, who is love and has shown us his countenance in Christ Jesus, who is his Son and our brother. Furthermore, both kinds of situationism include the danger of a pharisaic self-righteousness: "I have kept all the laws," or "I do everything with love."

Self-righteousness is bought at an even cheaper price with Mr. Fletcher's situation ethics. On page 147 of his book *Situation Ethics,* he writes, "Gone is the old legalistic sense of guilt and of cheated ideals. When we tailor our ethical clothes to fit the back of each occasion we are deliberately closing the gap between our overt professions and our covert practices. This is an age of honesty." Honesty? It is always easy to rationalize what we wish to do. Do we not all sometimes tailor the ethical clothes that cover our laziness, our lack of generosity, our utilitarian approach to other persons? But to seduce ourselves with such rationalizations is the subtlest and most destructive kind of dishonesty.

Bishop Robinson (*Honest to God,* and other books), Joseph Fletcher, and others are right when they insist on the Lord's word, "The Sabbath was made for man, not man for the Sabbath" (Mark 2:27). But when they apply this to all moral norms, saying "Morality is made for man, not man for morality," they show that they do not realize the true meaning of morality. There is a lack of discernment and distinction. Morality and moral norms are not mere laws made for man or imposed on man; they are the inborn laws of man's own being, the dynamic orientation given him in his original constitution, the laws innate in his very humanity.

I wholeheartedly accept the principle that "morality is for persons," but I would have reservations about accepting "persons are not for morality." Surely persons must never be sacrificed to an abstract moral code, but morality is something other than an imperfect moral code or a poor understanding of moral principles. In its proper sense, morality is the fullness of life and the development of the person; it is to the fullness and genuineness of love and responsibility that persons are called.

There may be fewer absolutes than we thought there were in earlier times, when detailed formulations of the natural law were too often misinterpreted as the law itself; but there surely are absolutes in ethics. Blasphemy and idolatry, the teaching of heretical doctrine against one's better knowledge, hatred for persons, false oaths, desperation, promiscuity, bestiality, suicide, murder, and similar perversions are always and under all circumstances against the nature and calling of man, against the true countenance of love.

A doubt may arise in some circumstances about whether or not a certain action falls under one of these absolute prohibitions. There can also be such a low degree of moral sense in some persons that they cannot understand why attitudes or acts against one of these absolutes is wrong. Invincible error on a certain level of moral underdevelopment is never excluded, even in very important matters, but such a moral underdevelopment is in itself a misfortune and often enough is the result of the sins of many.

For mature persons, the emphasis in Christian ethics, and even in natural law ethics, is not on those exceptional situations where acts which are generally called theft, suicide, murder, etc., may not fall under the more accurate moral definition of those sins. These problems can and must be studied, but unless they are integrated into a more dynamic perspective they will give occasion for a dangerous minimalism which could go beyond the licit; that is, against the real dignity of persons. The important moral question is whether the person would be facing toward the goal of man's vocation to "be all goodness," or away from it.

True Christian personalistic ethics recognizes the prohibitive absolutes, but its concentration is on those commandments which express the loftiness of man's vocation. The Christian sees the commandment "Love one another as I have loved you" (John 15:12) as an absolute in the sense of a commanded goal toward which everyone must constantly strive, even though nobody can achieve its total fulfillment on earth. It is an absolute that each person must make a serious effort to grow in an understanding of the order of love and the mediations of love. This means that we all have to work toward an ever better, more common, deeper knowledge of Christ, in whom God has manifested his countenance, his goodness, and the lofty vocation of all men.

13

THE ETHICS OF
VALUES

I N THIS century, especially in Germany and France, there
has developed a school of ethics—the ethics of values,
Wertethik—inspired by a personalistic pattern of thought and
based on the method of phenomenology. Kant was an early
advocate of the ethics of values in opposition to the ethics of
self-perfection (*eudaimonia*). From psychology and phenome-
nology, this ethical theory derived a greater sense of discern-
ment and came to appreciate more man's desire for happiness.
The substance of its message is that personal fulfillment and
happiness will be the harvest of a genuine response to values,
which means a genuine relationship with God, neighbor, self,
and world.

The central norm of the ethics of values is the norm of the
right preference (never fully identified, however, with the
absolute good) in conflicting human situations and the con-
flicting desires of man. The two chief principles are: first, in
your fundamental options you always prefer the higher values

to the lower ones; second, in the concrete situation you may prefer the more urgent and vital option, but in such a way and with such an attitude as to make apparent your continued preference for the values which in themselves are higher in dignity and splendor.

The German followers of this school of philosophy and ethics use the word *Wert,* which is difficult to translate into English. The English word "value" is less precise. It can refer to many things, such as stock on Wall Street or a piece of jewelry in a shop; whereas *Wert* means that which bears its splendor in itself. In ethics, then, we mean by "value" something which man recognizes as possessing an inner or essential beauty that inspires profound admiration. It finds its highest perfection in adoration, where total tribute is given to God, whose splendor and love are in all his works.

While I have not adhered to the thought of any single master in this field, I am indebted to many. I have learned a great deal from Max Scheler, one of the great thinkers who developed the ethics of values. Of Jewish origin, he was a convert to the Catholic Church. There was great turmoil in his life, and in many ways his life ended catastrophically, but nobody can judge.

When he had lost his faith, and his friend Werner Schöllgen, who had been with him since student days, came to him and tried to convince him with his own words and his own magnificent books on the *eternal* in man, he responded with a pitiful revelation. "With my whole heart," he said, "I wish to believe in this God of love, but I cannot believe that this God, a holy God, would create such a beast as I am." And he explained what he meant: that he had betrayed his wonderful wife, leaving her for a sexually attractive girl. Each year after their divorce he wrote gentle letters to her admitting his injustice and telling her, "You are the only woman I revere." God, I think, will be merciful to him.

Scheler's greatest works are *Formalismus in der Ethik und Materiale Wertethik (Formalism in Ethics and an Ethics of Incarnate Values)* and *Das Ewige im Menschen (The Eternal in Man).* Parts of his work have been translated into English.

With him, as with Tertullian, defection from the Church does not affect the value of what he wrote as a believer, but what he produced after his defection is not much better than what Tertullian produced after he left the Church.

I learned much also from Dietrich von Hildebrand, who communicated deep insights in his early works *The Meaning of Moral Action* and *Moral Values*. In his excellent book on *Transformation in Christ*, there is a beautiful chapter on the readiness to change. We cannot but regret that the man who could write this would later write his *Trojan Horse*, which discloses a latent Platonism and makes it impossible to realize the history of salvation and the law of growth and change.

There was also Alexander Pfänder and, above all, Edith Stein, the great Jewish convert who became a Carmelite nun and died in the gas chambers of Auschwitz as one of Hitler's martyrs. She has combined, as Max Scheler, Dietrich von Hildebrand, and Alexander Pfänder have, the method of phenomenology with the philosophy and ethics of values.

In his ethics of values, Max Scheler insists that moral value is not merely a means of self-perfection, and here he agrees with Kant. But he disagrees strongly with Kant's assertion that the ideal ethical act is done contrary to all desires and represents a renunciation of joy and of personal fulfillment.

Scheler insists that each moral value has splendor and brings joy. In his wonderful article on the evaluation of virtue, he shows that the immense beauty of virtue lies in a spontaneous receptivity and response to the magnificence, the nobility, the value of man and of relationships among persons. For him virtue is not the business of self-perfection but is splendor on the countenance of man who is open to the hierarchy of values and who responds to the language of God as it is spoken in all his words and works and finally in his Word, Christ. It is joining Christ in his love for man. And this virtue bears on its shoulders joy, peace, beauty.

Scheler's ethics of values is responsorial ethics. All values, all degrees of nobility and beauty in God's creation, in mature man and his struggling and growing, are finally the language of God, and through their variety God manifests himself. The great value of the person is love, his capacity to hear and respond to the language of love.

I think that if Fletcher, Robinson, and others would approach morality not only from the viewpoint of decision-making but from the broader perspective of an ethics of value and of fundamental attitudes in response to values, their ethics of situation would manifest more continuity and orientation.

A personalistic value ethics is constantly confronted with persons in relationship with each other. "Value" is the beauty and authenticity of personal and personalizing relationships. For a believer, the fullness of authenticity, dignity, beauty of values, shines forth in Christ. He manifests the true countenance of love. A philosophical approach is unrealistic if it ignores this highest manifestation of "value," wherein all values can be grasped as reflections of love in all its dimensions. Christ is the "Value-Person" in his infinite love for the Father in heaven and for all men. Believing in him, we can realize that all values on earth are messages of love and appeals to return love.

The ethics of values show that it is nonsense to speak of unprincipled love. Love is true to itself; it manifests and preserves and gives meaning and fullness to the scale of values. And here Max Scheler emphasizes the fundamental principle of an ethics of value, which is the sacrifice of the lower value to the higher. Man recognizes that his desires are not from true love if they seduce to a betrayal of higher values and thus disturb the encounter of persons in truth.

A Christian does not cultivate economic values at the expense of personal ones. He does not sell his brother for a certain number of dollars, or exploit friendship for business. But he can use business for promoting genuine friendship among men. A Christian does not cultivate sex values and bodily beauty at the expense of his deeper beauty as a person before God and man; he sacrifices what is lower in value when it conflicts with higher values.

The final rule, as Max Scheler and Rudolph Otto teach, is the sacrifice to the Holy One. We test all action, all desires, according to the scale of values and do not prefer anything over him who is holy, who is the supreme value in person. "Good" is that love for all persons which we can offer to God in praise of his name.

There is a certain difference in tone between the *Seinsethik* and the *Wertethik*, the ethics of being and the ethics of values. The ethics of being can be excellent if its thinking and language are personalistic, but often it is only a "thingified" ethics. Its chief principle, "the action follows the being," is acceptable if being and striving toward fullness of being are understood from the viewpoint of persons and personal relationships, but woe if persons are submitted to an impersonal order of being and nature!

BEING-A-PERSON OR BEING-A-"NATURE"?

Among Catholic thinkers there has been a certain tendency to regard all being as on the same level, a trend that confused the discussion about birth control. The inviolability of the biological pattern (as understood according to prescientific ethics) seemed to be the absolute rule of action. The marital act was understood more as an "act of nature" than as an encounter of persons. But profound thinkers focused strongly on the different degrees of density of being: the density of being found in persons and the relationship of persons is of a different order from the density found in things or in impersonal life.

By itself the "ethics of values" tends to favor a more personalistic form of expression. Instead of saying that the final norm of action is the nature of being, we say that the final norm is value: the meaning and relevance for persons and their relationships. The scale of values and the urgency of a value are wholly determined by the dignity of each person and the community of persons in the presence of God. We do not, however, as some German philosophers of the *Wertphilosophie* did, disassociate the values from being. Where there is the greatest density of value in person, there is the greatest density of being, of existence. The ethics of values is, therefore, not in opposition but complementary to the ethics of being.

One more point should be made. As against the tendency of extreme situation ethics toward unprincipled, agnostic love, it must be reaffirmed that there are absolutes. Not everything can be done in the name of love. Some actions are destructive of genuine love. But, in natural-law teaching, we must not affirm more than it is in our power to affirm. We must not speak in absolute terms when we have only weak proofs for our convictions.

It must be recognized that imperfect definitions, when only the materiality of the act is considered, open the door to all kinds of exceptions. But my point here is this: there can be definitions in terms of values and there can be an evaluation of attitudes as mediations of love. Then we cannot say, for instance, that contempt of persons can be as good as respect for the dignity of each person. Gentleness, kindness, sincerity are absolute values; lack of sincerity is always opposed to genuine love and can never become a "mediation of true love."

We need this type of evaluation when questions arise, as, for example, about the spy in an earlier chapter: what is suicide? Sometimes there are probabilities on one side or the other that raise valid questions. There are cases of doubt about whether an action expresses the malice of suicide or not. We cannot, therefore, oversimplify absolutes in a legalistic way that allows for no exceptions from value formulas. We should look rather to the absolute *value* of respect for human life and responsibility for it.

Another example which was much discussed in the past can serve to illustrate the different approaches to a formalistic ethics of principles (read "inherited formulations") on the one hand and a personalistic ethics of values and attitudes on the other. When the sperm of a man is needed in order to make a diagnosis for certain forms of cancer, or for a fertility test when a marriage is threatened by sterility, it is a matter of medical ethics whether the sperm is to be obtained by massage. The immediate response of one school of moralists was that this is intrinsically evil, since it is masturbation.

This opinion found authoritative support in Pius XII.

Father Franciscus Hürth, whose advice Pius XII used to follow on most moral matters, wrote in his commentary (in *Periodica de re morali*) that for married people the natural and morally recommended way to obtain the sperm for a fertility test was the "use of marriage with a slightly perforated condom." In this way, a portion of sperm could be deposited in the vagina for "preserving the procreative function of the marital act," while the condom with the rest of the sperm could be delivered to the doctor. Thus, through a "natural use" of condom and marriage, there could be obtained what it would be "intrinsically evil" to obtain by massage.

The article *"Samenuntersuchung"* in *Lexikon für Theologie und Kirche* (Vol. VI, Freiburg, 1964), edited by Karl Rahner and Msgr. Höfer under the auspices of the German hierarchy, adopts a different approach. Explicitly referring to the utterance of Pius XII, it approves of massage as a licit means for obtaining semen for such tests; in such cases it considers marital intercourse with a perforated condom more distasteful and more frustrating to the persons concerned than a simple massage. (Incidentally, the recommendation to use a slightly perforated condom is difficult to square with the reasoning against artificial means of birth control, although this was far from the intention of Father Hürth, who, along with Father Vermeersch, was the chief drafter of the encyclical *Casti Connubii!*)

The crucial point here is the danger involved in the generalization of principles without any search for personalistic values and nonvalues. The use of a perforated condom is justified on the grounds that some semen is deposited in the vagina for "the procreative goal of the marriage." But the assumption was, in the first place, that the marriage is sterile! It is not the deposition of semen but the desired fertility itself which can serve the parental vocation of this couple.

Further—and this is the main point—massage as a means of obtaining semen necessary for a cancer diagnosis or fertility test is labeled "masturbation" without posing the question of "intrinsic malice" in terms of the value or nonvalue for persons. Is masturbation sinful because of the loss of semen or because of the pleasure which might accompany it? In my understanding of a personalistic ethics, the nonvalue of masturbation lies in the self-centered, immature use of sex for self-gratification, an attitude that does not prepare the individual for mutual self-bestowal in marriage. It is not the loss of semen or the accompanying pleasure but the arbitrary and selfish attitude toward one's own sexuality that is the "malice" or "nonvalue."

From this it seems evident that massage to obtain semen, in the context of a necessary fertility test or cancer diagnosis, has nothing to do with the *moral* nonvalue of masturbation. How this procedure might affect the individual person is, of course, a psychological question which is not without relevance to moral judgment. Assuming that no harm is done to the person, the moral question is whether it is in accordance with the scale of values if a person accepts the somewhat unaesthetic and unpleasant aspect of this sort of massage for the sake of health, the preservation of life, or the desired fertility of a marriage. This, it seems to me, is the kind of perspective that fits into a personalistic ethics.

CONFLICT OF VALUES AND DUTIES

In their statement commenting on *Humanae Vitae,* the French hierarchy applied the vision and principles of the ethics of values to the problem of birth control. "Contraception is never a value in itself" (No. 16 of the declaration). A static ethics of values would then conclude that it is always sinful. But the French bishops, when there is a conflict of duties, see the matter in the perspective of a scale of values which includes the urgency of duties. The higher and more urgent values—to preserve unity, fidelity, harmony in the marriage, or the bodily and mental health of the mother—can justify that minimum of interference with the biological processes which seems necessary for the preservation of the higher goods. The bishops rightly insist that the human person can be confronted with conflicts of duties and values in all areas of life. They also remind their faithful that the traditional moral theology was not unaware of this perspective.

A personalistic ethics of values has to pay great attention to the hierarchy of values and to discernment for resolving the conflicts. One of the important questions will always be: what will be the effect of a certain solution on the development of everybody involved and on the whole community of persons?

DYNAMIC ORIENTATION OF AN ETHICS OF VALUES

Some exponents of an ethics of values have adopted a rather static concept of morality. This may be caused by their concept of values as ideals similar to the "ideas" of Plato. But an ethics is of little avail if it does not give fullest attention to growth and possible conflict in growth.

It is an absolute for Christian ethics that all have to strive to fulfill the great commandment of the Lord, "Love each other as I have loved you," "Be all goodness as your heavenly Father is good." On the other hand, it must be shown that certain attitudes are in striking conflict with the exigencies of true, Christlike love. But then the greatest attention has to be given to growth within the limits of the person's possible and real freedom and insight. The fundamental option of the right direction and honest striving count for more than actual achievement. Only gradually can the human person— especially if he comes from a confused environment—grasp the higher values and the sacrifices which are demanded in the scale of values.

Moral guidance cannot be given by looking only to the heights of platonic values. We have to know the human person with all his complexities. Depth psychology can offer us important lessons with regard to the real possibilities. Even if it is a matter of absolute values, ethics must not be "imperative" in the manner of absolutism; what is called for instead is a humble effort to let the value enter into the mind and heart of the person at the right moment and through that little door which alone may be available.

I remember a rather touching insight into the depth and complexity of human nature. An elderly priest in Rome who was very ascetical and severe with himself, as well as with others, became somewhat senile during the last weeks of his life. To the brother who took care of him he would say, "Brother, bring my secular clothes; I want to go out and enjoy my liberty at least once in my life." But then, in a routine way, he would give his own response. "But, brother, what would the people of the Holy Office say if I were seen in secular clothes and enjoying my liberty?" So the nature of man is in all his ways, all his desires. The object should not be to expel nature, which will ever return in spite of us. We can expel selfishness but not the nature of self. What revealed itself in such strange fashion during the man's later days may well have been a cause of tension and overcompensation in earlier days, or may have been caused by an all-too-rigid approach in many daily problems.

An ethics of values that can motivate and inspire love, joy, and enthusiasm for all that is good leads to better psychological health and greater freedom than an abstract ethics of laws and imperatives or of "nature" and being.

As I understand it, natural-law ethics is personalistic and existentialistic, and thus an ethics of values and growth. We must not, in pastoral counseling and education, impose what is abstractly the highest ideal; we must not even, under all circumstances, hinder what in itself is against the full ideal of love. But we must always help people to discover the ever-greater dimensions and ever more beautiful horizon of goodness, and help them to find out each time what the next possible step should be to lead them in that direction. Christians will be prepared to meet difficult situations involving conflict if they can discern the height and urgency of different values.

14

HISTORICITY AND
NATURAL LAW

ALL thought bears the stamp of the thinker's world and his own personality. It cannot be otherwise, since man comes to knowledge through his experience of the world into which he is born. Because of this, we cannot consider natural law without taking into account the situation or context in which various theories with regard to it evolved and were formulated.

Today, more than ever in the past, we have greater knowledge of man's history: his progress, his various cultures, and the breadth or narrowness of his experience at any one time or place. And we know that only when we have placed theories of natural law within their historical and cultural contexts can we properly evaluate what is abiding in them—and therefore applicable to our own times—and what represents earlier limitations of knowledge or cultural legacies from the past.

THE CONTEXTUAL ELEMENT OF NATURAL-
LAW PHILOSOPHY IN THE PAST

Before the days of the Roman classical jurists, Greek philosophers of the natural law took as their starting point their observation that there were certain elements of morality and law common to the different nations united within emerging Hellenistic culture. Later on, the Roman lawgiver, bearing in mind his unifying role, tolerated among the various tribes, cultures, and nations which the Romans brought under their "peace," wide differences in customs and concepts of justice. He knew that he must make allowances for variety in order to keep the nations under Roman rule, but he maintained certain common elements amid the variety.

Under the civilizing influence of this common law—the *ius gentium*—the various parts of the Roman empire were unified and great cultural, economic, and social progress was made. Horizons loomed far beyond the narrow ken of the early Romans and subject peoples. There was a cultural encounter of broad dimensions. Yet those who formulated a theory of natural law at that time could not conceive how small this world around the Mediterranean Sea would appear to later generations. Neither could they realize to what extent their natural-law thinking was conditioned by their desire to civilize under the Roman peace. But we know today that this political motivation was dominant and impressed itself on most of the formulations.

Another historical source of natural-law thought was cosmopolitanism, the idea of a world-wide city, common to the Stoics and throughout Hellenistic culture. This was the environment in which the first Christian missionaries worked. Some admirable theories about the natural law were elaborated just at the time when the Greeks were growing out of the cultural limitations of the polis or individual small town and embracing the wider concept of an integrated culture with a common language and a common ethical understanding. Alexander the Great's empire also included captive nations with various cultures. The short period of political unification was followed by a most fruitful cultural exchange. Therefore, in the Hellenistic ethics, natural-law theory was much less exposed to the danger of becoming a political ideology. It was a co-reflection of many subcultures meeting in a great awareness of the unity of the human race.

However, no one realized that this encounter of cultures in the Hellenistic melting pot was only a modest beginning compared to later epochs—our own age, for instance, when we can compare existing and past cultures so easily. Neither could theorists of natural law realize at that time how much the old culture and its tradition depended on the philosophical thought of Plato and Aristotle, and on a particular stage in economic and social development. They thought they were expressing pure natural law, but when we read their works today, we find remnants of their limited cultural outlook in almost every line.

The Greek and Roman classical ages, which saw the formulation of natural-law theories, were ages of heroic growth, expansion, and planning. Greek culture finally subdued even the Roman conquerors, and the latter subdued not only the many nations around the Mediterranean but also nature itself by means of great feats of engineering. Yet they could not even dream of how many ways and to what extent man would later subject nature to his planning, including even his own biological nature. They could not yet explore the dimensions of man's own nature in his relation to the world in which he lives and which he can mold, because the dimensions of human nature with which man today is familiar were unknown to them.

Works on the natural law are influenced by the historical context of the thinker to such an extent that, when we read today what they considered to be the nature of man, we can at once reconstruct the cultural, sociological, and religious environment of the particular thinker or group of thinkers.

One sees this even in the broader approach adopted by theorists of the seventeenth, eighteenth, and nineteenth centuries. At the time of Hugo Grotius (in Dutch, Huigh de Groot, one of the great Protestant natural-law thinkers),

Dutch ships were sailing all over the world and the Dutch people boasted that they knew the whole world; yet, from their works on natural law, we can reconstruct the small world and special environment of Antwerp. And we can see that the theories appeared meaningful because they were essentially related to realities being faced by men at that time and in that place.

Again, we note the great difference between formulations of the natural law during the period of romanticism, reflecting a sharpened sensitivity to the diversity of cultures and the influence of the French Revolution; and, on the other hand, formulations of the era of the Restoration, characterized by the idea of a "Holy Alliance." Since conservatives then believed that the prerevolutionary order would be restored, they adopted the approach of rationalism, which, with its abstract, unhistoric thought about an unchangeable objective order of nature, is alien to the perspective of salvation history. The too-static concept of natural law simply reflected the static character of a society and Church which opposed any changes as long as possible.

During the last century, most natural-law theories were influenced by the rationalism of the era. Today we must be aware of the opportunities and dangers of another trend: our present thinking is unavoidably a reaction to the tremendous dynamism of modern society, either by way of swimming with the mainstream without critical discernment, or by way of violent opposition to any change.

This whole stream of contextual history makes it clear that we do not have *one* natural-law theory in the Church. We have to recognize this fact and be cautious. Failure to recognize the existential context of natural-law formulations peculiar to different epochs and cultures could diminish the value of our approach.

This contextual element raises some important questions. We have to ask in what sense we can speak of continuity in such matters. As Christians and as modern men, what do we really mean by natural law? Can we speak about an unchanging, abiding element? What is objective truth in natural-law theory?

THE ETHICAL MEANING OF NATURAL LAW

I present here my own personal understanding of natural law. Not all will agree with it completely; some may not agree with any part. Some, too, would prefer to use an expression different from "natural law," and I have no objections to discarding the term if this will facilitate communication with other Christians and the secular world. However, we have also an obligation to continue dialogue with those who are familiar with the vocabulary and meaning of a tradition as expressed in the natural-law theories.

In ethics, natural law means the very nature of man in his concrete, historical reality, insofar as he has the capacity to understand himself, his calling or vocation, and the meaning of his person and his relationship to God, to fellow men, and to the created universe.

There is actually only one historical order: the order of salvation. It is not accurate to speak of a strictly "natural" order apart from the order of salvation. We do distinguish natural law from the actual revelation of God's design in the call to salvation, but the distinction involves only the way in which we come to a knowledge of his design. The way known as the natural law means that, through the capacity of our mind, through shared experience and reflection, we grasp what is good, right, and just. The other way is through God's self-manifestation through his prophets and truly inspired men, culminating in Christ, who is his final Word to mankind.

Beyond our own effort of self-understanding through shared experience and reflection, however, we realize that it is, nevertheless, still God who discloses what the eyes of reason can gradually see. Whether through the use of reason or through the Word of God revealed in the Bible, the source of our self-understanding is, therefore, always God, who manifests his design in different ways.

Strictly to the natural law, therefore, belongs everything pertaining to the realm of human experience and reason without a special "supernatural" revelation.

This definition of natural law immediately discloses aspects of continuity and great variety. It is fundamental to natural law, and belongs to the idea of humanity and the unity of mankind, that man has the capacity to ask himself what he is and what he is meant to be and do. But he has this capacity of self-understanding only in community with other people, not in isolation. There is no possibility of self-understanding in isolation; it has to be in communion with others. Therefore, we insist upon the expression "shared experience and reflection."

There have been horrifying experimentations with a child brought up without contact with other people. The child remained incapable of language, without love, and without "natural law," since his capacity for love and intelligence did not develop. Only in communion can man open his eyes of reason and develop verbal and vital communication. So when we speak of natural law, it is not only what *my* reason sees, not my reason in isolation; it is the experience and co-reflection of man in community, enriched by culture and dialogue, and enriching his own environment. Communication and communion is a basic element of continuity and progress.

WHERE DOES THE HISTORY OF NATURAL LAW BEGIN?

The whole evolution of the universe led up to the appearance of mankind, but man's beginning as such can be traced to the appearance of *Homo sapiens,* the species of man with whom we are concerned when we speak of natural law. Man begins to exist as a fully human being only when he develops beyond the stage of merely caring about his nourishment, protecting himself against the natural elements, and learning to use tools. He is not yet *homo sapiens* until he comes to exist in a human way, as an outgoing person who has developed some capacity to reciprocate love and thus to become conscious of a moral problem. When he receives love from others and starts to reflect upon what he is and ought to do or should have done, especially in relation to his fellow men, then he is truly man, historical man.

In a religious sense, the history of man—the history of salvation—begins only when man realizes that God has revealed himself to the eye of reason and therefore man must honor God and render him homage. Human history and the basic experience of natural law begin when man can adore God and love his neighbor.

I have no theological objections to accepting the theory of polygenism, whether from the viewpoint of human solidarity or with respect to the biblical doctrine of original sin. But if tool-making and tool-using beings actually developed from different biological starting points, I would not count them as members of the one mankind until they can honor God through mutual love. The very nature and unity of the human family throughout history reside in this basic capacity to acknowledge God the Creator, at least implicitly, through respect and love of fellow men. In other words, man's true nature and the natural law starts and has its focal point in the capacity to love and to adore. However imperfect the element of knowledge may be, this marks the beginning of the real continuity of wisdom and religion.

The Epistle to the Romans (1:20) says that from the beginning of human existence God has disclosed to the eyes of man's reason his everlasting power and deity and has given man the capacity to render thanks. I consider the most fundamental part of natural law to be this religious event of God disclosing himself to human reason in the things he has made. So natural law is not something besides religion; man's capacity for religion is its very foundation.

But while we consider the history of mankind as beginning with the moment when human persons could love each other and thus render thanks to God, we cannot say anything about the concrete way in which the first man and woman came to grasp this fundamental calling. Was it first an explicit act of worship in response to God's revelation, or was it a life response in mutual love that honored God?

We have, above all, to distinguish between a definite

existential realization and a capacity to conceptualize it in abstract terms or in adequate images. To realize and to conceptualize are two different things. One may be able to conceptualize but not to realize; another even more developed person may realize but not be able to conceptualize. Cardinal Newman was quite insistent about this point of vital "realization," meaning an existential grasping.

Natural law begins before philosophizing about the natural law, but it does not begin at all until man has to some extent been able to reflect on his experience and can "realize" that he is bound by some moral value. First comes the vital experience of man who realizes his fundamental freedom and responsibility, man who can entrust himself, who can worship, and who realizes something of brotherhood. Philosophy is a later stage.

Although I am convinced that natural law has its foundation in the existence of God, who is love and who discloses himself to man, I would not dare to assert that the reality of natural law entered into history only with explicit faith in God and with the structure of thought and life that is explicitly related to it.

Neither history nor philosophy can enlighten us about whether man's first experience was one of religious awe or of a sense of moral obligation toward his fellow men. In the present day, there are some who first experience religious awe and from this discover a deeper relationship with man; and there are others who develop a great moral sense with regard to fellowship and go on from this to religion. So we do not know how God began with humanity, nor can we predict the ways in which he will lead the individual person.

A sense of moral responsibility may have preceded the sense of religious awe and dependence. The fundamental recognition of natural law may have been a spontaneous experience of relationship to one's fellow men without realization of the radical implication that all men could really be fellow men. Men of the Stone Age could not yet have realized much about the broad fellowship of mankind all over the earth, although they could experience fellowship within a small

group. But, again, it must be said that there is a great differ-
ence between a human experience which includes such a
principle, and the capacity to conceptualize the tremendous
experience of human love.

Once man was awakened to humanness in love, awe, admira-
tion, gratitude, he would try to understand all this more
clearly. This might be called the real beginnings of "natural-
law thinking." However, this should definitely not be confused
with abstract thinking of the rationalistic type.

THE EXTENT OF THE HISTORICITY OF MAN'S NATURE

Rationalistic understanding of the natural law starts with
abstract principles which have been found always to reflect a
certain truth. This truth allows some limited variety in its
application according to varying circumstances, but it discloses
nothing with regard to the historical background of its first
formulation. We have here a static approach to man's being,
in utter unawareness of its historic context.

Our approach actually starts with real man as a historical
being, with a real capacity to understand himself in his
essential relationship to his fellow men, to the world around
him, to self, and to God. From this beginning, we see some
continuity in man's increasing power to grasp the meaning of
his destiny.

According to this view of natural law, there is a twofold
source of profound dynamism. First, although the subject is
always the same nature of man, the man of the Stone Age
and the man of the modern scientific era are totally different
in their interests, languages, horizons, consciences, and powers
to conceptualize life. Their worlds provoke altogether different
kinds of thinking and questions; their cultural backgrounds
have very little in common. Even their biological makeup
and their psychological reactions are different. Second, as man
begins to shape his world he himself changes, and his basic
capacity of self-understanding and of self-expression grows
and undergoes remarkable changes.

The *Constitution on the Church in the Modern World* (Article 5) stresses the fact that the profound changes in our world are leading to a transition "from a rather static concept to a much more dynamic vision of life." Speculation about the natural law has to make this transition too if it wants to remain relevant for modern man. Without this deeper awareness, we cannot even understand the tremendous variety of past history, about which we now know more than any previous generation.

To man in history, truth has been revealed gradually to the degree that he can receive its message. From the viewpoint of God, it remains always the same design, but man sees different aspects and degrees of the whole truth. Ours is not a humanity that from the beginning has had a collection of well-formulated natural-law principles in its pocket to be applied to a variety of situations. So it is not simply a matter of different applications of eternal principles. No eternal principle has been formulated from the beginning, because God does not formulate his knowledge in human language. He himself, the living God, is eternal truth. Yet there are true principles which, by means of man's way of thinking and experiencing and his degree of self-understanding, guide changing man through a changing world in genuine continuity of life.

When we speak of natural law, we cannot overlook the essential historicity of man as a part of that law of being, as a part of man's destiny. He is ever an existential person, being and becoming "more-being" at the same time.

Historicity permeates all mankind and all ages of man, both as person and as species. A child is a person with intellect, experience, free will, a sense of duty, and humor. The degree and expression of these qualities, however, differ at ages two, five, fifteeen, thirty, eighty. In the history of mankind there is a similar progression. There is an infancy, a childhood, and an adolescent period of humanity that should constantly grow toward fuller maturity. However, there can also occur terrible decay in some cultures.

PERSPECTIVES OF MAN IN SALVATION HISTORY

Not only for primitive man but for Greek and Roman thinkers too, it was impossible to imagine the dimensions of the historicity of man. Like Indian philosophy, Greek thought shows a great lack of awareness of the historical dimension. They were not aware at all of the history of salvation as disclosed in the Old and New Testaments. In fact, we ourselves are only now beginning to realize the tremendous perspectives, possibilities, consequences, and responsibilities inherent in salvation history and in the historicity of human nature.

In our consideration of moral questions, we are more conscious than men of earlier centuries that we have to be content with our historical heritage, the limited nature of our language, our limited possibilities of thinking, and our approaches to human problems. We have to build on what we have received. But, on the other hand, we have to face new, undreamed-of possibilities of changing our heritage, interfering with biological, psychological, and eugenic processes, and shaping our future.

Historicity belongs to the constituent structure of man and therefore to the constituent structure of natural law. It belongs to the existentialist human vocation. Man's power of thinking, his degree of freedom, sexual determination, faculties of joy, all are affected by his time and place in history.

Incidentally, we should not forget this faculty of joy. The ancient Greek philosophers had an excellent criterion for determining what man is. Man is *Homo risibilis,* a person with the capacity to laugh; and he is not fully human without it. It is a fundamental characteristic of man to have humor. Yet man's whole environment, culture, and human experience can change this capacity to laugh—either diminish it or enlarge it. Only through a comparative study of the variety of cultures can one realize the extent to which freedom or the limitations of freedom can affect humor in all its phases.

ONE HUMAN FAMILY, ONE HUMAN RESPONSIBILITY

The entrance of the Jewish and the Christian faiths into history, with their typical understanding of the oneness of salvation in view of the one Creator and Father and the one Redeemer, has greatly affected history itself, man's understanding of it, and man's thinking about the natural law.

These faiths, and the experiences accompanying them, have contributed to the fact that believers and unbelievers alike take it for granted today that all men belong to the same human family and have a common responsibility. Even the question whether we all have a common origin from one man and one woman no longer seems the fundamental question, for all are one in the sight of God and therefore are called to live according to this unity in diversity. The unifying factor is the one design of the Creator and Redeemer of all, he who calls all men in one hope.

At the present time, this unifying factor may be the most important approach to natural law. The tremendous concern for solidarity and oneness among many unbelievers may also be the most efficacious way to faith in one Father of all. We experience this when we realize that if we do not resolve our problems together, the whole world can be consumed. This consciousness grows. It may be one of the most fundamental religious and moral experiences of our time.

GROWTH IN NATURAL-LAW THINKING

Not only in the matter of existential personal ethics, but also in natural-law thinking, we must see the "law of growth" at work. Many problems typical of past history cannot arise again, and we of this century, on the other hand, cannot make formulations which will have validity for the man of the twenty-third century. Natural-law thinking, therefore, contains as an absolute element the need for a continued effort. A humanity which stops short with the formulations of a certain era is worthy to be buried in a museum.

For me, one of the most amusing experiences when working on the Preparatory Theological Commission of the Vatican Council was the continual warning by the secretary of the commission that, when drafting all documents, we should constantly bear in mind that our formulations must be as valid for the year 3000 as for the year 1959!

But if we really want to communicate truth, we have to speak to men in the language of their own times. We must listen to them and speak to them about their concerns and questions. Conscience unites us with all men in the search for truth. Since the Christian community did not receive all answers from the very beginning and does not yet have all the answers or the whole truth, natural law has both the possibility and the need for growth through shared human experience and co-reflection.

Toward the end of his teaching on earth Christ said to the apostles (John 16:12), "There is still much that I could say to you but the burden would be too great for you." Fidelity helps us open to growth in understanding. Humanity and the Christian Church will always be faced with new problems and will have to reflect constantly on past heritage with a view to present experience and responsibility for the future.

Historicity of natural law and the constant need to broaden the horizon are conditioned by the wonderful truth expressed by Christ: "My Father has never yet ceased his work, and I am working too" (John 5:17). In Hebrew the words for "work" and "word" (*dabar*) are the same. The ongoing creation, the ongoing history cannot be met by stereotyped formulas of natural law. The dynamism of our age requires an attitude expressed by the Lord: "When, therefore, the teacher of the law has become a learner in the kingdom of heaven, he is like a householder who can produce from his store both the new and the old" (Matt. 13:52).

In our natural-law thinking, man is history, has a history, and shapes history, progressing from infancy to maturity.

15

NATURAL LAW AND REVELATION

F OR man, historicity means *growth of consciousness* or awareness of the continuing evolution and development of the whole universe, and particularly of man's ascent to the point OMEGA. Man uses his reason when gathering experience and reflecting and co-reflecting on this growth, viewing the past in an effort to understand what is involved in his task of mounting to an ever-higher degree of consciousness in the future, through increased socialization, complexity, and personalization.

My effort here is to relate to the natural law this growth of consciousness, reflection, and co-reflection on the part of the person and humanity.

Our precise question is, How is the growth of consciousness and co-reflection about ethical questions related to revelation and the history of salvation whose center and culminating point is Christ?

DIFFERENT FORMS OF REVELATION

Must we disregard revelation when thinking on the level of natural law? Certainly not! To do so would be to falsify our thinking about man's real nature, because it would not be historical man's thinking. We would hardly stop short of self-destruction if we tried to develop reason by dissociating it from the highest form of consciousness, namely, faith in God who reveals himself and his loving design for man.

Yet we distinguish between revelation and natural-law thinking in that the "natural law" is within the realm of insights accessible to human reason without "supernatural" revelation. But we also see that man himself, in his very nature, is a revelation of God, and the whole universe proclaims his glory and manifests his loving design for man. So we really differentiate between two forms of revelation. The difference lies in intensity, consciousness, and gratuitousness. What comes to man in one form, through his experience, gifts of intellect, capacity to love, to be astonished, and to admire, is a message, a revelation, through the creative word and renewing action of God. On this level, we speak of "natural law," meaning a perception, through shared experience and reflection, of what God reveals through his creation and through the very nature of man as seen in his culture and ethical heritage.

From this we distinguish revelation in the history of salvation, which came through men who were touched by God in a special way and inspired by the Holy Spirit.

It is my personal opinion that our understanding of this special type of revelation must not be confined to the Jewish-Christian traditions. We have indications of this in the Old Testament, where sayings of sages other than Israelites were honored. Even the "donkey of Balaam" prophesied, meaning probably the humble people of Israel and other nations as well. So we may acknowledge an inspiration or special presence of the Holy Spirit in holy men outside the Jewish people and beyond the boundaries of Christianity but according to God's design and related to Christ.

GROWTH IN CONSCIOUSNESS AND FAITH
IN CHRIST

We believe—it is a most fundamental article of our faith—in the uniqueness of revelation in Christ. We do not put Mohammed, Zoroaster, Buddha, or others side by side with Christ. Christ is *the* revelation, *the* message, and *the* messenger. He is the perfect image of the Father and has disclosed to us everything he has received from the Father (*cf.* John 15:16).

In order to avoid any unnecessary misinterpretation of what we are talking about here, I want to draw attention to our limited approach. The question is not: What is the full message of Christ? Of course, Christ is infinitely more than a teacher and genius of ethical values, and faith in him is more than a new ethical outlook and strength. Our present question is: How is our natural-law thinking or our growth in moral consciousness related to the entrance of Christ into human history?

The ethical prophets of the Old Testament had already enriched and purified the moral heritage of Israel and of all humanity. But the entrance of Christ changed human history by bringing totally new elements into human experience. In one way or another, either positively or negatively, the presence of Christ in history is felt by everyone.

Before he came, natural-law thinking was that of man not yet confronted with the fullness of redemption. Man was ever inclined to an unredeemed personalism of self-preservation. This is true not only of the attitudes and decisions of individual persons but also of systems of thought. But since his coming, man's reason can see more clearly the pitfalls of self-centeredness and can find a deeper understanding of what the human person is really meant to be.

Christ's life, his personality, his witness, and the witness of his followers opened moral and religious values to the intelligence of earthbound man in a way that can no longer be ignored. Through his manifestation of the true countenance of love, through the teachings of his Church and the witness of his true followers, in whom the features of love are recognizable, his ethics of love has become a part of the experience of human history.

When men are confronted by persons and communities who live a fully developed moral life as a result of their faith in Christ, this has great influence on their own way of thinking. It affects the direction and capacity of their self-understanding, even before they come to an explicit faith in Christ. Take, for example, the biblical truth of the *kairos*, and the eschatological virtues of vigilance and constant readiness. These are, and must be, reflected in genuine natural-law thinking by people who meet Christians, act as Christians and are able to communicate their thought. Neither believers nor unbelievers can avoid a confrontation with this contribution to the understanding of human life. This attitude becomes "open to the eyes of reason" as soon as it is a reality of human history.

Natural law means the sharing of existential experience and reflection by persons. So man, once he has come in contact with Christ, cannot look upon his total experience as if Christ did not exist. The believer cannot follow a whole pattern of thought alien to Christ unless he is a victim of schizophrenic thinking.

It would be an error, however, to intimate that when these persons have been enriched and changed by Christ their thinking is no longer their own good reasoning and experience. Men of faith develop even greater capacity to treasure up experience and to reflect on their own being and experiences. Natural-law thinking of Christians is, therefore, intimately related to the history of salvation and situated within it.

DIALOGUE WITH ALL MEN IN FULL AWARENESS OF FAITH IN CHRIST

One can go still further. The whole pastoral *Constitution on the Church in the Modern World* of the Second Vatican Council is an effort to communicate with all men of normal intelligence, normal ethical experience, and good will. In other words, we want to share all our insights and experiences and search for truth and goodness together. In this communication, however, the Church keeps her own identity. She uses arguments which should be accessible to the intelligence of all well-disposed men; but before she offers any arguments she tests them in the light of the Gospels.

It was a rather exciting experience to be on the Theological Commission during the Second Vatican Council and see how the council Fathers and theologians wrestled with this problem. There were many theologians, conservatives and progressives, who thought that if the Church wished to have a dialogue with the world of today, she must remain on a fairly philosophical level, acting like a wise grandmother who, having gathered a store of human experience and philosophical wisdom through many centuries, now wants to share this store with men of other ethical and philosophical experiences.

It was chiefly due to the efforts of men like Archbishop Wojtyla of Krakow—a very gifted personalistic thinker who has now become cardinal—that the commission and the council were finally convinced that this would not be a dialogue between the Church of Christ and the modern world but only a dialogue between a wise grandmother and other more or less experienced people, or between a group of ecclesiastical philosophers and other friends of wisdom.

If the Church wishes to foster a dialogue, she has to present herself in her own identity as a Church who submits her thinking to the judgment of the Gospels and seeks her way in the light of the Gospels. However, in that light, we are to use our reason and profit from human experience and insights, and we must be aware of the deepest desires of the human heart. I think this decision was vital for the future development of natural-law thinking and teaching in the Catholic Church.

IS FAITH BASED ON A PARTICULAR PHILOSOPHY?

This renewed outlook toward natural law, with a deeper awareness of its existential involvement in Christian experience and therefore in all human experience, will hopefully also have an impact on seminary training. The dichotomy between a philosophy unrelated to faith and a theology which seemed sometimes like a bare superstructure, or an external addition to human life and thought, was a sign and a cause of the gap between religion and life. Since seminarians had to prepare for the study of scholastic theology with two or three years of scholastic philosophy, many thought that faith is based on a certain type of philosophy.

A few years ago we had a two-week-long institute in Toronto for professors of moral theology on "Renewal of Moral Theology." At the end of the institute, one of the participants asked, "On what philosophy, then, will we base our faith?" The answer was, "On none." Christ did not send his apostles to Athens. They did not go out with a certain philosophy but with the Good News and with good human common sense.

At one time I gave a series of lectures in Austria and made a similar remark about relying too much on Aristotelian philosophy. A professor of philosophy in a major seminary, a great admirer of Aristotle, protested. He thought that the Church should not imitate Christ in the one matter of teaching his apostles theology without first demanding a philosophical training. He considered this a unique dispensation which should never be repeated. Then, apparently thinking he had understated his case, he added that the people of the Old Testament, and even the apostles, would have made better progress in the understanding of the law and the Gospel if they had been trained in Aristotelian philosophy!

During recreation we had some fun with this "mixed marriage"—which our friend considered indissoluble—between Aristotelian philosophy and theology. Father Raimann, a popular preacher and writer who had not lost his sense of humor even after years in Hitler's concentration camps, said, "Father Häring, I cannot see how you can get a divorce or an annulment if this marriage was authorized with a dispensation from the impediment *disparitas cultus*" (a marriage between baptized and unbaptized persons). We saw two possible ways out of the difficulty. First, it can be proved that the hierarchy rejected the idea when Thomas Aquinas announced that his theology was wedded to Aristotle instead of to Plato. Second, there is the encouraging disagreement between the Roman Rota and the Holy Office (Doctrinal Congregation). The Rota thinks that a marriage between a Christian and a non-Christian, given the dispensation, is a sacrament, but the Holy Office thinks it is not a sacrament; therefore, perhaps the Holy Office can grant a divorce and permission for a new marriage—under the condition, however, that the new one is between two Christian partners!

At all times Christian thinkers must seek for a vital exchange and unity between faith, and shared human experience and insight, since we have to work for an organic vision that includes morality and loyalty to the regulations of the Church and secular society. But a scale of values and a hierarchy of perspectives must always be observed. It was an unfortunate "mixed marriage" when the theology taught in seminaries was based on Aristotelian philosophy and when evangelical morality was seen in the light of Stoic ethics or canon law.

The council decree on seminary training (*Optatam totius,* Article 14) declares: "In the revision of ecclesiastical studies, the first object in view must be a better integration of philosophy and theology. These subjects should work together harmoniously to unfold, ever increasingly to the minds of seminarians, the mystery of Christ, that mystery which affects the whole history of the human race."

With this in mind, we can liberate natural-law theories from their isolation and partial alienation. The goal cannot be to belittle human growth in consciousness, shared experience, and co-reflection, but rather to see all this in the broadest perspective of *salvation through faith.* The honor we owe to God does not allow us to narrow the vision of his revealing and saving action by placing human consciousness, experience, and reasoning in opposition to God's action and revelation or on the same level with it.

At the same time, we must be concerned for a better communication with all men in the common search for truth. To this end, we have to come to that fullness of vision which places the growth of human consciousness in a genuine perspective of faith.

GOD'S CALLING AND REVELATION
THROUGHOUT HISTORY

The vision and vocabulary of the Bible are personalistic not only when it speaks about eternal life but also when it speaks about secular events. God lets himself be found by those who seek him. When man strives for a deeper understanding of love, this itself is a sign of God's gracious and dynamic presence.

Growth in consciousness, experience, and co-reflection draws men together and thus opens more vital horizons for faith in the one God and Creator. The Bible (*e.g.,* Matt. 25:35-46) tells of those who actually found Christ in their suffering brothers whom they fed and clothed and visited. They are within the saving realm in which God reveals his love, even though they may not be in direct contact with explicit faith in Christ. This, too, is a lack of growth in consciousness. However, it does not separate them finally from God's self-manifestation when they truly open themselves to the call that comes from the Other and respond in love.

In every genuine experience of personal love gratefully received and generously reciprocated, we must see an element of revelation coming from God and indicating the way to him. The existential search for ethical truth, in its readiness to act accordingly, is a saving event insofar as it is brought home by the final self-manifestation of God in Christ's love.

It was theologically wise to exclude from "salvation through faith" all those forms of natural-law ethics which convey a whole establishment of pride, domination over others, and impersonal submission to natural processes. But a genuine natural-law ethics, one that searches for better knowledge of men in all his relationships and for better discernment of all genuine forms and mediations of love, must be seen in the light of God's self-disclosure in all his works throughout history. Man, as image and likeness of God, is a message of God. If he discloses real love to his neighbor, then he becomes an accredited messenger of the one who is love and who, in final analysis, calls for nothing other than love.

Throughout the whole history of mankind, there is, however, a conflict between the saving disclosure of love and man's free refusal to rise to a better understanding of his humanity. This is damaging to all mankind. Only insofar as man's greater consciousness leads to a better discernment of the true "nature of human love" can he remain in the mainstream of salvation history.

Natural law, as an ethical force and liberating norm, is never a final acquisition. Man never possesses it. As soon as man complacently reposes on his intellectual and ethical achievements, he closes himself to the ongoing history of salvation. Only a dynamic approach to natural law provides that openness which is man's responsive attitude toward God's revelation. Even in the hands of churchmen, scribes, pharisees, theologians, canonists, and bishops, natural-law principles can become a "whore," an expression of a lack of faith, a rejection of the great mystery of love, if there is no readiness to learn and unlearn and reconsider everything in the light of Christ's redeeming and healing love.

A rationalistic natural-law philosophy that draws its logical conclusions from formulas, without first studying the phenomenon of man, is disobedience to the Lord of history and in striking contradiction to the total reality of revelation and faith. The man of faith constantly listens and searches for better understanding. Similarly, natural-law ethics bears the signs of the *analogia fidei*—the marks of an attitude characteristic of faith—only if it makes use of all our resources of investigation before drawing conclusions in the forms of ethical principles and imperatives.

The day before the *Constitution on the Church in the Modern World* received its final approval, the conservative-regressive group of bishops at the council in the *Coetus Internationalis* (bishops who have played an important role in promoting the present malaise in the Church) charged that the document was loaded with phenomenologism and evolutionism. They were scandalized by the fact that an authoritative

Church document dared to study the present situation in the world! The same group was bitterly opposed to the concept of the "signs of the times." They seemed to think that the Church has all the answers from past tradition or can draw the necessary conclusions from well-known "principles." Such a closed system of natural-law ethics has no place for the kind of receptivity which distinguishes the man of faith, who, like Abraham, leaves everything behind and entrusts himself to the Lord by going out into the promised future.

IN THE LIGHT OF THE GOSPEL

Christ is the final Word of God to the world. If a "post-Christian era" does become an actual fact for the millions, this will represent a terrible regression. Anyone who looks on such an era as "progress" is denying Christ and all that faith in him has meant to the world. No event in history can make Christ superfluous; he remains the cornerstone. But our Christian era is also the time between the first and the final coming of the Lord.

Christ is the key that opens the total meaning of history, which must be viewed as an ongoing process in which the covenant between God and mankind unfolds itself ever more visibly. New events, new knowledge and power are constantly being granted to man. Openness to Christ demands openness to all this, but in such a way that Christ's revelation and commandment of love give final meaning to all the insights of the natural law. If a thesis of natural-law ethics contradicts the personalism revealed by Christ, it stands unmasked as error.

The discussion about organ transplantation can illustrate the point. A group of Roman theologians (Fr. Hürth, S.J., Fr. Bender, O.P., and Fr. Hering, O.P.) tried to obtain from the authorities a solemn condemnation of all forms and experiments of organ transplantation. Their chief argument ran like this: Catholic natural-law teaching has always condemned self-mutilation as intrinsically immoral; organ transplantation from one living person to another involves self-mutilation. Therefore, for an objective evaluation, it does not make an essential difference whether the organ which a person decides to have removed, without any reason of personal health, is thrown on the dunghill or used for saving the life of a son or daughter, because "the good goal cannot justify the intrinsically bad means; namely, self-mutilation."

Pius XII read the address drafted by this group, but alerted by his own sensibility and by other theologians, he cancelled the key paragraph. After his death, almost all theologians returned to their previous view that, when making a responsible decision to sacrifice an organ—*e.g.,* a kidney—for another person, there is no malice involved as in self-mutilation. (One of the few exceptions is Ermecke, editor of the moral theology of Mausbach. He continues to advocate the same arguments and maintains a materialistic view of each part of any human action, instead of looking to the total meaning.)

It is more reasonable to argue, as most modern men do, that organ transplantation is not ordinarily immoral. There is no good reason why renunciation of an organ or interference with a biological function is justified by the needs of one's own health, while the same thing is labeled immoral when done out of unselfish love for another person and without harm to one's own personality (the capacity to live a full life of love for God and neighbor). Human co-reflection should become especially effective in the light of Christ, and churchmen should have been the first to see the fallacy of the other argument, since their thinking is supposedly formed by the paschal mystery and the Gospels. "There is no greater love than this, that a man should lay down his life for his friends" (John 15:13). "A grain of wheat remains solitary unless it falls into the ground and dies, but if it dies it bears a rich harvest. The man who is selfishly concerned for his life loses his true self" (John 12:24-45).

In the first edition of my book on moral theology (*The Law of Christ,* 1954), I mentioned the matter of transplants and said that it poses no problem for a moral theology based on the imitation or following of Christ. But after Pope Pius XII spoke (although not as emphatically as Father Hürth and the others had wished), I changed the wording, saying that there was now a problem, since conflicting opinions existed in the Church—one opinion opposed to the morality of transplants, and the other favorable to the conviction of many theologians and laymen that transplants can be licit and beneficial if the necessary conditions for a responsible decision are present. After the Pope's death, I returned to my former view, as did most other moralists.

This example reveals something about the relations between the magisterium and natural-law thinking. We of course have to have respect for the magisterium and should not simply say that there is no problem. When the Pope speaks differently, there *is* a problem. The teaching of the successor to St. Peter has to be taken into serious consideration. While this is done, however, a more intimate knowledge about the circumstances and full context in which a papal document is issued can be of great help in interpreting it with greater clarity and sensitivity.

The example also points up the fact that the authority of the magisterium will be greater (and hence more "authoritative") if it is really based on a wide range of thinking and discussion. If the Pope relies on only a handful of advisers belonging to one school of thought, then his "authority" when teaching about the natural law will inevitably suffer—as has been the case with regard to such matters as usury, torture, the burning of witches, the castration of choirboys (who sang in the Sistine Chapel), and the like.

MAGISTERIUM AND THE NATURAL LAW

When Paul speaks about natural law in the Epistle to the Romans (1:19-27, 1:31-32, and 2:14-16), he is not referring to a teaching of Church authorities on natural law. He is speaking about people who, although they have not the revealed law or the guidance of rabbis, are not bereft of all moral insight. "When Gentiles who do not possess the law carry out its precepts by the light of nature, then although they have not the Law they are their own law, for they display the effect of the law inscribed in their innermost being" (Rom. 2:14).

In the biblical perspective, natural law is the inner direction of the conscience and not something imposed by any teaching authority. It is unthinkable to tell people within the Church or outside the Church to ignore their own consciences in favor of certain formulations of the "natural law," since natural law is not the legislation of any human authority but the sincerity of man searching for truth, the inner impulse to follow one's own sincere convictions. Within that searching, of course, are shared experience and co-reflection.

But the Pauline texts, and indeed the whole Bible and human experience, draw our attention also to the fact that man is exposed to tremendous dangers of self-deception if he is not completely sincere. Even more, man must be aware of the need for redemption with respect to his own reflection on human experience and his inner dynamism, which can be deeply disturbed by sin. "Their conscience is called as witness and their own thoughts argue the case on either side, against them or even for them" (Rom. 2:15).

One of the noblest and most urgent tasks of the teaching office of the Church is to sensitize people with respect to the need for having sincere convictions and expressing sincerity in their thoughts, actions, and communications. Any attempt to impose some noninfallible doctrine on people against their better convictions will inevitably lead to a breakdown of sincerity, a resort to hypocrisy, or to a lessening of personal efforts toward achieving a deeper understanding.

Not only the average layman but those in authority particularly should be fully aware that they too are in need of redemption regarding their understanding of the natural law. While sincere and docile attention ought always to be paid to those in authority, all must be prepared to accept mutual correction. Throughout Old Testament times and for as long as the Church has existed, God has sent his prophets to challenge high priests and kings.

It is held by some that Christ's promise of special assistance to the apostles also includes a divine assurance that the magisterium will be free from any error or even defect when teaching ethical norms within the natural-law sphere, but neither the Bible nor history favors such a view. The faithful are guaranteed absolute certainty only when confronted with the deposit of faith entrusted by Christ to his Church. Many aspects of morality which are accessible to shared human experience and co-reflection are affirmed in the Bible. However, we often have to take a closer look to discover whether the Bible is guaranteeing divine revelation to moral laws valid for all time or incorporating imperatives that are relevant and vital only for a certain age or a certain stage in human development.

Vatican II teaches that "this infallibility with which the divine Redeemer willed His Church to be endowed in defining doctrine of faith and morals extends as far as extends the deposit of divine revelation, which must be religiously guarded and faithfully expounded."* Bishop Gasser, the official spokesman for the doctrinal commission at the First Vatican Council, declared before the plenary session of that council that it was the explicit intention of the doctrinal commission not to include in the definition of infallibility those theological matters not belonging directly to the deposit of faith.** The Council of Trent, too, when speaking about the indefectibility of the Church, includes only the doctrine of Christ "which through the apostles came to us."***

All these texts surely do not favor the opinion of those Catholic theologians and bishops today who say that the Pope could pronounce infallibly on matters of the natural law that do not form part of the divine revelation disclosed by Christ. They are free to think this way if they wish, but they should not try to impose their dubious "maximalist" views on others. The uniqueness of faith obliges a Catholic not to speak about "obedience of faith" when it is only a matter of natural-law doctrine and not at the same time a doctrine taught by Christ and contained in the apostolic tradition.

* Vatican II, *Dogmatic Constitution on the Church (Lumen Gentium)*, Article 25.
** T. Granderath, S.J., *Geschichte des Vatikanischen Konzils von seiner ersten Ankündigung bis zu seiner Vertagung.* Freiburg i.B. 1906, III, 476.
*** Council of Trent, Sessio IV, Denzinger-Schönmetzer, No. 1501.

The people of God as a whole have a duty to be docile to the Lord of history and therefore to be open to all morally relevant experiences and insights. But we must all recognize that the Spirit works through whomever he wills when assisting his people. God does not oblige the faithful to anything which has relevance for salvation without bestowing his gracious help upon them at the same time. The Church, therefore, cannot be without the assistance of the Holy Spirit when it is an important matter of bearing fruit in love for the life of the world, but members of the Church can be partially lacking in docility and obedience toward the grace of the Holy Spirit. One is indeed not docile to the Spirit if one is not open and docile toward the insights and experiences of other people. It is an undeniable fact that under both the old and the new covenant even those in authority were not always spiritual men but sometimes were persons lacking in humility, docility, and wisdom. Even very spiritual and saintly men have erred when they did not have access to the shared experience and co-reflection of mankind.

Neither the whole visible Church, with all its members, nor the magisterium has any monopoly in matters relating to moral experience and insight based on human knowledge. The magisterium can be said to be faithful to the divine mandate and docile to the Holy Spirit to the extent that it is ready to use all available means to come to an ever more adequate understanding of such matters. The divine mandate does not dispense anyone from the necessity of informing himself and recognizing the limits of his information and competence.

Because of their respect for an upright conscience and their own sincerity of conscience, all Christians, especially those in authority, "are joined with the rest of men in the search for truth and for genuine solutions to the numerous problems which arise in the life of individuals and from social relationships" (*Constitution on the Church in the Modern World*, Article 16). The task of the magisterium is not to teach natural-law doctrines unknown to men through shared experience and co-reflection but rather to help the faithful to discern and integrate into a perspective of faith and redeemed love what humanity already knows by way of experience and reflection.

The magisterium can and must pronounce on assertions made in the name of reason if these assertions contradict the doctrine of salvation which the Church received from Christ. In this case, the arguments must be taken from the deposit of faith; in such cases it is not just a question of the "natural law."

Since by definition natural law means "what is visible to the eyes of reason" (*cf*. Rom. 1:19), the magisterium cannot dispense itself from the need for furnishing convincing arguments, based on human experience and shared insights, for what it declares to be the natural law. Otherwise, it is not educating toward maturity or acting on the specific level of the natural law. Therefore, in cases when a truth of the deposit of faith is not involved, either positively or by way of contradiction, official teaching about the natural law must be thoroughly based on what it has learned after canvassing all possible views, before making its integrated decision. The teachings of the magisterium will acquire more moral stature and carry more weight if the limit of certainty or tentative character of an approach is clearly and humbly pointed out by the magisterium itself. God's authority, or a divine mandate, ought not to be invoked when convincing arguments are lacking.

The task of theologians and of the magisterium is not met merely by repeating and inculcating an unchangeable mass of formulas and concepts. They must always be faithful to the living God and of service to living men. Here, also, the faithful householder will "produce from his store both the new and the old" (Matt. 13:52). The chief concern of everybody must be for what is expressed so marvelously in the ethical prophesying of the Old Testament and, above all, in Christ; namely, achieving an integrated approach in which the focal point is the manifestation of God to all persons and communities and the human response to this manifestation.

Whether we speak about revelation or the natural law, we must recognize that there exists no such thing as "pure nature" or a "merely natural" order of things. Man discovers his real nature as God intended it to be, when he breaks away from all fetters of selfishness, taboos, and all impersonal attitudes in order to be truly free for genuine, responsible love. This is the road toward which God's revelation, in all of creation and above all in Christ, is leading the persons who constitute his human family.

16

NATURAL LAW IN THE
DIALOGUE BETWEEN
BELIEVER AND
NONBELIEVER

A DEEPER understanding of natural law can provide an important focal point where all men—Christian and non-Christian believers, as well as nonbelievers—meet to collaborate in achieving a more brotherly world and peace on earth. Such a deeper understanding should be the Christian contribution to such a collaboration. Moreover, if the natural law is carefully distinguished from the deposit of faith (while nevertheless remaining well integrated in a Christian view of the oneness of history), it can become a valuable means of pre-evangelization: a way of speaking about the living God, even though his name is never actually mentioned.

On the other hand, without adequate preparation, study, and carefully drawn distinctions, talk about the natural law could also help promote, more or less explicitly, the idea that "God is dead." If we offer men today natural-law formulas couched in static language which leave no place for the innate dynamism that God has assigned to man, then we will not only fail to communicate with them but, in effect, be denying the existence of a living God who works through and with mankind.

NATURAL-LAW THINKING IN THE FELLOWSHIP OF CHRISTIAN BELIEVERS

The true Christian believer, above all, depends on the Word of God, that is, on that undeserved supernatural divine revelation which attains its fullest expression in Christ. This provides him with fundamental help in his moral life, since faith gives him a deep insight into and a right attitude toward moral decisions. But faith cannot resolve all moral problems, especially new and urgent ones. No believer, therefore, is dispensed from the effort to use all the forces of heart and mind at his disposal to try and understand more profoundly his own role and mission in the world.

The above distinction between the two channels by which God communicates his love and truth to man—divine revelation and man's intellectual effort—is clearly recognized by the Christian believer, but he also sees these channels in their wholeness and synthesis, as different avenues toward truth but within the single order and history of salvation. It is always the one God who leads man both to an understanding of himself and to a realization of the loving intention of his Creator and Redeemer for him.

For the believer more than for the unbeliever, human reason and experience are an important source of moral knowledge. The believer recognizes the ultimate dignity of human knowledge: in the last analysis it is God himself who speaks through continuing creation and through the hearts of men, God himself who has endowed man with the power to grasp gradually the meaning of the created world and discern his own role in that world.

In this sense, natural law is based on the self-revelation of God to the human intellect through the work of creation. The intellect faces a living and loving God and becomes blessed with an adoring outlook toward him rather than concentrating on an impersonal collection of abstract norms. "All that may be known of God by man lies plain before their eyes; indeed God Himself has disclosed it to them. His invisible attributes, that is, His everlasting power and deity, have been visible to the eye of reason ever since the world began, in the things He has made. There is therefore no possible defense for their conduct; knowing God they have refused to honor Him as God or to render Him thanks" (Rom. 1:19-21).

When we think of natural law according to this typically religious attitude of the Christian believer, our first emphasis is always on God's manifestation of himself in all creation, including man and his ability to understand what God wishes to convey through experience and intelligence. Only secondarily do we consider man's own effort, which we describe as an effort to open himself in active response to God's manifestation, by using all the forces of mind and heart, reason and pondering on experience, and especially by the sharing of insights.

The rules of ecumenical dialogue, as well as our own concern for a genuine religious attitude, oblige us to put the emphasis on God's initiative and to see clearly that man's effort can have importance for salvation and wholeness only to the extent that it is inspired by God's gracious presence and initiative.

In dialogue with Protestants, we should be very sensitive about their concern for the principle "salvation by faith alone and by grace alone." We rescue this truth from the narrowness in which fundamentalists have confined the terms "faith" and "grace"; we do insist that man's openness to fundamental moral and religious truths, his readiness and capacity to share valid experience in genuine co-reflection, has its deepest roots in God's loving intention to be found and known by human persons, whom he created in his own image and likeness and whom he calls together in human history.

Discussions about natural law in the fellowship of believers, therefore, should lay stress on the openness which characterizes faith and the response to God's gifts (grace). Its chief content is God, who reveals to our reason not only abstract norms and values but something also of his own attributes and intention for man, which give the final meaning to moral conduct.

The Christian knows well that the sinfulness of mankind has obstructed and darkened man's receptivity to this self-manifestation of the Creator; but redemption, accepted by man, exercises a liberating power on the human intellect and on moral experience. To the extent that man, acting responsibly and in fellowship, opens himself to the redemptive light of faith, the eyes of reason will be cured of this blindness. Natural-law knowledge will then become a greater and more beautiful reality within the realm of faith.

The fellowship of believers, and especially the teaching ministry of the Church, will submit human experience and all thought about the natural law to the light and judgment of faith. They must also conceive of it in a Christocentric way. "The Word was with God at the beginning, and through Him all things came to be; no single thing was created without Him. All that came to be was alive with His life" (John 1:2-4). Christ "is the image of the invisible God; His is the primacy over all created things. In Him everything in heaven and on earth was created . . . the whole universe has been created through Him and for Him" (Col. 1:15-16).

The truth of salvation, revealed by the living Word of God, provides a wider context for and sheds greater light on all possible insights pertaining to the realm of natural law, that is, the realm of human experience and co-reflection.

NATURAL-LAW DIALOGUE BETWEEN CHRISTIANS AND OTHER BELIEVERS

Christians and non-Christians can communicate with each other the truth that "has been visible ever since the world began to the eye of reason." When doing so, however, we may neither exclude nor deny the possibility that some persons and groups among non-Christian believers have developed deeper insights about some of the truths revealed by the Creator and accessible to man's reason and have conformed their conduct according to these insights better than some Christians have. On the part of the Christian believer, therefore, dialogue must mean that he is ready to learn from others, to listen thoughtfully to them before proposing his own message.

Dialogue about the natural law, with respect to those

things which can be known through human reason, must be conducted in faithfulness to the identity of the partners. Both partners, Christian and non-Christian alike, must distinguish between truths which seem to be accessible to reason and human experience, and those aspects of religion and ethics which the Christian accepts as part of an original, special divine revelation. However, men of all religions should not forget that in the past many things were asserted in the name of revelation that were later unmasked as mere prejudice or presumption. Think, for example, of the alleged "direct power" of the Roman pontiff over kings and rulers in the Middle Ages!

The Christian need not try to hide the way in which he correlates faith in revelation, faith in Christ, and his own understanding of human nature. Indeed, by disavowing his own identity, by totally separating his thought about natural law from the structure of his faith, he invites the danger of having it become a deadly issue. On the other hand, he must avoid any assertion about natural law which cannot be shown as "visible to the eye of reason." A believer can lead the dialogue only to the extent that he is completely open to the new aspects and problems of life.

NATURAL-LAW DIALOGUE WITH
THE NONBELIEVER

The same rules must be applied, though in a different way, to dialogue about the natural law between believers and nonbelievers. In a serious dialogue, everyone must know and respect his own identity. However, in some cases, the identity of the partners may be somewhat ambiguous. There may be Christians who, from a conceptual and institutional point of view, call themselves believers but manifest, at least to some extent, the structures of unbelief in their way of thinking and acting. Conversely, there are sometimes "anonymous Christians" who call themselves nonbelievers, although the structures of their life and their views about the natural law and the values or ideals to which they have committed themselves reveal their support for the very structures of faith: an openness to the message and appeal of the Thou, dedication to absolute values or ideals in a personal way, concern for the value of the other person, etc.

The difficult question is really this: since our natural-law thinking is rooted in a structure or pattern of thought leading to belief, how can we communicate meaningfully with persons whose structure of thought leads to unbelief? The best answer seems to be that there is rarely a sharp line between white and black, and almost invariably some meeting place can be found. With any earnest partner in a dialogue about moral values, we can generally find some concern for the good, which in our eyes is a bridge to the attitude of faith, even though the conceptual framework may be oriented toward atheism.

For our part we should make clear that, although our thinking is integrated with belief, this does not mean that we are less earnest or less aware of the limits of our insight. Above all we must try to avoid any oversimplified identification of our own convictions or opinions with faith or with the Gospel message. The *Constitution on the Church in the Modern World,* Article 43, notes that, "often enough the Christian view of things will itself suggest some specific solution in certain circumstances. Yet it happens rather frequently, and legitimately so, that with equal sincerity some of the faithful will disagree with others on a given matter. Even against the intentions of their proponents, however, solutions proposed on one side or another may be easily confused with the Gospel message."

NATURAL-LAW THINKING AS A POSSIBLE SOURCE OF UNBELIEF

Vatican II has very serious words about typical unbelief. "Undeniably, those who wilfully shut out God from their hearts and try to dodge religious questions are not following the dictates of their consciences. Hence they are not free from blame" (*Constitution on the Church in the Modern World,* Article 19).

But besides nonbelievers who "wilfully shut out God from their hearts," there are numerous other nonbelievers who are in search of the living God but who encounter difficulties on the way. And some of these difficulties may be due to believers. Article 19 continues, "Yet believers themselves frequently bear some responsibility for this situation. For, taken as a whole, atheism is not a spontaneous development but stems from a variety of causes including a critical reaction against religious beliefs, and in some places against the Christian religion in particular. Hence believers can have more than a little to do with the birth of atheism. To the extent that they neglect their own training in the faith, or teach erronenous doctrine, or are deficient in their religious, moral or social life, they must be said to conceal rather than reveal the authentic face of God and religion."

One must frankly admit that the way in which believers—especially some theologians and pastors—have proposed natural-law teachings has sometimes contributed to unbelief, or at least been a cause of serious temptation to those already wavering in their faith. When theologians and churchmen generally attempt to impose something as an absolute teaching of the natural law, alleging arguments which do not carry conviction with the best and most intelligent minds, the authority of the natural law is diminished in the eyes of earnest nonbelievers, and wavering believers are confirmed in their wavering. Doubts will also arise about other doctrines claimed by the same teachers to be divine revelation, so that some will think, "They teach as doctrines the commandments of men" (Matt. 15:9).

If natural-law doctrines are proposed in an authoritarian manner, without supporting evidence or without recognizing the limits of such evidence, most intelligent people will feel that not enough attention is being paid to the experiences, needs, and insights of men today. If only a narrowly selected group of "laws of nature" are alleged as evidence, or if these laws are not subordinate to the exigencies of love and mercy,

law of nature and of God, then great harm was done to faith itself.

Men of the present scientific age must never be given the impression that natural-law teaching relates only to the nature and reasoning of men belonging to a pre-scientific epoch. If we look at human nature as it appeared to be under totally different historical circumstances and as expressed in a totally different vocabulary, and if we then maintain the absolutely binding character of this kind of "natural law," people will think that our God did actually die at the end of the pre-scientific era.

Moralists who wish to be totally "safe," by merely repeating "immutable" principles or offering solutions advocated in the eighteenth century, or by "resolving" new problems in basically the same framework, should make a severe examination of conscience to discover how many good moral norms have become incredible because they have been justified by arguments unmeaningful to our times.

In earlier formulations, of course, these were aspects of abiding truth; but stereotyped formulations, taken out of their historical context and merely repeated, not interpreted, do not convey any abiding truth about man and the Lord of history. How much Stoic psychology, biology and medicine of Galen and other early thinkers, vestiges of Roman and Germanic culture, and jurisprudence of the absolutist age in Europe, still remain in our manuals? Even the official teaching of the Church has sometimes been more handicapped than helped by this type of natural-law thinking.

This reexamination has to be done in freedom and responsibility, and with mature respect for the teaching office of the Church and a sense of continuity with the best efforts of the past. It must be an effort by the whole people of God. Wisdom should discourage us from throwing away all moral norms as soon as any doubt arises as to the validity of arguments used in their formulations. Perhaps some norms will be not only reformulated but also strengthened through free discussion and by the use of all the insights of the present scientific age. But respect for truth and honesty, and ultimately concern for the credibility of the Christian message, oblige us to recognize more fully the limitations of our natural-law arguments with respect to several serious problems today.

Toward this end, we can be helped even by atheists if we take seriously their difficulties, questions, and adherence to some human values.

NATURAL-LAW DIALOGUE AS
PRE-EVANGELIZATION

The Second Vatican Council shows us a way in which natural-law thinking, integrated into the total witness of the people of God, can be an important contribution not only to the welfare of mankind but also to the strengthening of hope and faith in the living God. "The Church knows that her message is in harmony with the most secret desires of the human heart when she champions the dignity of the human vocation, restoring hope to those who have already despaired of anything higher than their present lot. Far from diminishing man, her message brings to his development light, life, and freedom" (*Constitution on the Church in the Modern World,* Article 21).

Natural-law thinking today must be focused especially on concern for every human person and the building up of a society in which everyone is respected and feels his dignity protected more effectively when he himself contributes to the dignity of neighbor and the welfare of all. Not only in its solutions but in its whole mode of expression, this thinking and teaching about the natural law must be personalistic. By "personalism," however, I do not mean self-centered individualism but rather the personalism of I-Thou-We, the social personalism of the human person who "cannot find himself except through a sincere gift of himself" (*Constitution on the Church in the Modern World,* Article 24).

If Christians show clearly, by their way of thinking and by their actions, that their eschatological hope is contributing effective energies to the building up of a more humane and brotherly world, then natural-law teaching too may lead in an authentic way to the question of the living God. A common action of believers and honest nonbelievers "for the betterment of this world in which all alike live" (*Constitution on the Church in the Modern World,* Article 21) cannot be realized without sincere and prudent dialogue, but the contribution of believers toward this common action will foster such dialogue to the extent that it evidences a complete sincerity.

When Christians dedicate themselves with idealism and realism to the future of the whole of mankind, and especially to those who are victims of discrimination, and when their dedication shines forth as a natural harvest of their own Christian hope, then those so-called nonbelievers who are so generously working for a spirit of brotherhood and respect for human dignity will more easily find the hidden presence of God in this Christian hope and selfless dedication.

The privileged sphere where the Christian faith and the secular world of today are encountering each other is on the ethical level: over concern for each man's dignity, unity in diversity, peace and development, and responsibility for the mankind of today and tomorrow. To the extent that believers really show that their faith in God opens them to others and gives them a clearer direction toward the future, secular man will recognize that they believe in a God who is and who will be.

Perhaps Harvey Cox has something similar in mind when he speaks about God in terms of "an open future," even though it seems at times that the open future of this world and of mere human hope in social and political concern is, for him, the Godhead. But for Christians this concern for present opportunities and for the future does not mean de-emphasizing or dismissing their hope in life everlasting and their faith in a living God who is beyond human history. Instead, they manifest that God is present in human history as well as beyond it, and because of that, their faith and hope lead them to use to the full the present opportunities for the witness of hope and brotherhood in justice and love.

In order to take seriously our common history on earth,

Christians need not forget about the beginning and fulfillment of the history of salvation. They need only to make clearer, even in their natural-law thinking, that they take very seriously the historicity of man because they believe in the God of the living.

In view of the present crisis of faith and in view of some forms of modern atheism, the natural law has to be rethought and reformulated along more personalistic and existential lines, and with the greatest concern for openness and continuity in the historical process. And finally, natural law must be rethought with more awareness of the limits to the reasons we have advanced in several areas of debate. If we try to teach more than we actually know about the nature of man, we are not making our message of the Lord and Creator of human nature credible.

But if faith fully awakens Christians to that sincerity of conscience which "joins them with the rest of men in the search for truth and for genuine solutions to the numerous problems which arise in the life of individuals and from social relationships" (*Constitution on the Church in the Modern World*, Article 16), then there will be an existential bridge between believers and all those nonbelievers who are searching for truth and love.

17

THE DYNAMICS OF
GRACE AND FAITH

CHRISTIAN personalism operates in a dynamic continuity.
To understand both the dynamism and the continuity,
we must recall the biblical ethics of grace, faith, the law of
growth, and finally the law of continual conversion.

Evidently, when we use the word "law" in the affirmative
context of grace, faith, growth, it cannot mean something
restrictive or imposed, or something that focuses attention
on a boundary line. What it describes is a totally new vision, an
urgent orientation of the Christian toward the loftiness of the
Christian vocation in response to God's gracious and dynamic
presence.

THE LAW OF GRACE

In the Bible, grace is the presence of God himself and our
joyous recognition that God is turning to us, showing his

countenance, making known the secrets of his mercy, his justice, his encompassing love. It is the dynamic attraction of his love as manifested in all his works and gifts but particularly in Christ Jesus, who is Grace in person. (The Greek word which we translate as "grace" can be interpreted also as "charm," and could be understood in this context as the magnetism of the presence of God who is holy.) In our response, we turn our face to him in joy and wonder, because he first has turned his face to us and has chosen us to receive his love and to communicate it to our fellow men.

This reality is above all *gospel,* good news, messianic peace. It carries with it a profound sense of obligation, but the obligation of gratitude and faithful friendship, not of an imposed command. "I call you servants no longer . . . I call you dear friends" (John 15:16). The character of law and obligation exists only to the extent that the self-centered Adamitic man still lives on in us and does not fully realize the attraction of God's love; but prohibitive law must never be severed from the dynamism that directs us forward. Thus obligation, law, and morality are but the other side of the coin of grace, taking hold of us, liberating us more and more for God, who is attracting us to him and drawing us together.

Grace is the way God teaches us through all the signs of his goodness. His presence directs our path, becomes our orientation and our life-giving law. In his Epistle to Titus (2:11-14), Paul speaks of grace as teaching us in the context of Christ's gentleness. In Christ, God's gracious presence dawns upon the world with healing for all mankind. It urges us forward, teaching us to renounce godless ways and worldly desires. disciplining us to live a life of temperance, honesty, and godliness in our time. Thus we embrace the time of salvation in which we live, and come to an ever-clearer recognition of God's presence and of the demands his love has laid upon us.

Grace should never be thought of as a thing, or simply as an instrument or means for attaining virtue. This relationship with God cannot be thought of as utilitarian; it is wholly personal, a loving dialogue, an I-Thou relationship that reflects the relationship between the Father and Son in the

Holy Spirit. Through this most personalistic and existential reality, we are liberated from the fetters of selfishness, enabled to be outgoing and to find the "We" in our brethren.

The law of grace is never static. Its dynamism is always in the direction of a fuller life through an ever more profound knowledge of Christ and thus through a deeper knowledge of God and of our brothers. We emerge from the narrowness of our "I" and see the loftiness of the Christian vocation "to be all goodness just as the heavenly Father is all good" (Matt. 5:48). We become oriented to the height, the depth, the length, and the breadth of the love of God.

Those who concentrate on boundaries, limits, and prohibitions, and attach only secondary value to spiritual theology and its law of growth, believe more in Adam and sin than in Christ and holiness. But the man who responds to grace sees the opportunities God offers him, rather than the threat of the devil. His affirmative orientation leads him away from the dangerous boundary, shows him the fruits of self-centeredness in their misery and sinfulness, and the difference between their harvest and the harvest of the Spirit.

We all know, as St. Paul did, "the kind of behavior that belongs to the selfish nature: impurity, fornication, indecency, a contentious temper, selfish ambitions, dissension, intrigue, jealousy, drunkenness, and the like" (Gal. 5:19-20). And whoever lives his life in thankful acceptance of God's graciousness and makes this the rule of his creative freedom knows that Paul is not limiting genuine freedom when he warns, "as I warned you before, that those who behave in such ways will never inherit the kingdom of God" (Gal. 5:21).

Situationists who refuse to worry about these texts should at least realize that the kind of freedom they propose is not the same as Paul was fighting for in the Epistle to the Galations. Through Christ, he knew what genuine freedom and true love are, and he rejected everything that by its very meaning expresses slavery to the selfish self. It is unthinkable that he would have said about adultery, rape, intrigues, that they are "sometimes good, sometimes bad." They can never be a response to God's gracious gifts.

A true appreciation of grace teaches us to "walk in the Spirit and you will not fulfill the lusts of self-indulgence" (Gal. 5:16); for when man is led by the Spirit he is freed from the chains of selfishness. Then he is no longer under the law, because he has outstripped the law. He has overcome those attitudes against which the prohibitive law stands. The Pauline vision shows that the opposition is not between nature and grace or between body and soul; it is the life-giving Spirit against a narrow self-centeredness; it is man being freed from "un-nature" through gratefully accepting God's grace as the rightful rule of his life.

Thomas Aquinas sums up the teaching of the Bible and theological tradition when he says that grace of the Holy Spirit is the very heart of the New Law and of the freedom of the sons and daughters of God. Grace gives a new mind, sets a new order and perspective in which the redeemed person sees everything in the light of God's gifts and God's call.

In this new order the human passions and desires are neither extinguished nor diminished but rather are intensified when they are purified by the fire of love. Their energies are collected in the joy, enthusiasm, and gentleness of those who, by crucifying their selfish desires, allow the Spirit to fill their hearts and minds and to guide their wills. Grace turns us from self-seeking to self-giving and makes us sharers in God's creative freedom.

The classic formulation of the law of grace is found in Gal. 5:29: "Since the Spirit is the source of our life, let the Spirit direct our course." We are redeemed if we no longer ask, "Must I do this?" but look instead to the gifts of the Holy Spirit and ask, "What can I render to the Lord for what He has given me?" For everyone who is taught by grace, the chief emphasis is on those commandments that direct us toward the heights: "Be compassionate just as your heavenly Father." "Love one another as I have loved you." In these commands, the gentleness of Christ is manifest as an attractive and encouraging power.

NATURE, GRACE, REDEMPTION

A theology based on the history of salvation pays little attention to distinctions which pose a man's real calling against a "pure nature" which can be thought of by man but is not part of God's design. It does pay much attention, however, to the difference between man's unredeemed nature and his redeemed nature, between the I-possessed personalism and the I-Thou-We personalism.

The distinction between nature and grace served to make us aware of the undeserved goodness of God, and indeed we can never praise God's grace enough; it is beyond all expectations and all merits of creatureliness, since through it we share God's own goodness and love. But we should look upon grace not as something that is added to a nature but as something that restores man, brings him back to God's original design, gives him a new direction, new dignity. It especially gives him the right perspective toward all God's gifts, which are then directed toward the salvation and welfare of mankind, the whole family of God.

The concept of redemption does not allow for two separate departments, one bare nature and the other additional grace. Grace means synthesis, integration, wholeness. It is man's total openness to God, rendering thanks for all things and using his gifts for his greater glory. Here is true Christian existential personalism: the total existence of a man liberated from slavery and savagery, redeemed, who in gratitude and fraternal love returns everything he has to God, who gives him a share in his life, love, and creative freedom.

Christian personalism is a response to grace and is, therefore, very different from a selfish and anguished concern for self-perfection. It calls for a trustful and creative commitment to God's own design, his plans for the universe which proclaims his glory, and it is directed to the service of man. This is a dynamic program. There is no room in it either for a rigorism that does not revere God's mercy and his creativity which makes everything unique, or for a minimalism that scorns God's grace and aims only at the boundary line.

Under the law of grace, morality is a creative fidelity and a constant striving. It often means that a man must come from afar, but essentially it means that a man, having perceived that God has turned his countenance toward him, sincerely turns his face to God and makes his way to him.

THE LAW OF FAITH

Faith is a dialogic, responsorial relationship between God and man; it is not just an operation of the intellect, not—as one American bishop so unfortunately defined it recently—"a catalogue of things believed."

Seen according to biblical personalism, faith is man's person-to-Person trustful communication with God. God opens man's eyes, ears, heart, mind, and will, and manifests in Christ Jesus the mystery of his love, the truth of salvation. Faith receives Christ, and in him and with him responds to the Father in joyful receptivity and creativity to the saving truth. In its very nature, faith is praise of God.

Christian morality is based on the faith by which man is justified. Through our reception of saving truth and our total response in surrender to God, faith bears fruit in justice and love.

There were some who resisted this message of the Gospels even in the days of the apostolic Church. Many Jewish Christians saw Christ chiefly as one who came for the glorification of their "law," their holy rule and customs. Such zealous conservative Christians were still seeking justification through observance of a certain code and wanted the chief emphasis to be on laws. St. Paul opposed them vigorously and became the great messenger of salvation through faith. He and his followers were accused of breaking down morality, not only by the Pharisees but also by these Christian preachers, moralists, and canonists. But Paul rebuked them: "Do we therefore, through faith, destroy morality? By no means! Rather we give morality ['law'] a firmer foundation" (Rom. 3:31).

Insistent emphasis on laws weakens morality by weakening its foundation, which is faith, joy, love, worship. By putting morality on the firm foundation of faith, we are strengthening it, showing the dynamism of God's saving truth and of the Gospels, which give us an affirmative direction.

It is by progress in faith, through an ever-deepening knowledge of Christ, that morality progresses, for in this way we see the higher demands of the Christian message. A deeper knowledge of Christ leads us to act more joyously and more vigorously in accordance with the word of God. To the extent that we act upon the level of knowledge we have already received, we become wiser and reach a still more vital knowledge of faith. The Sermon on the Mount, which so happily proclaims the saving truth, concludes with this clear statement: "Whoever hears my words and acts upon them is like a wise man" (Matt. 7:24).

Faith is manifested to us in the community of the faithful to the extent that this community is vital; therefore, our grateful acceptance of the saving truth is also a commitment to the community of faith, a constant appeal to contribute to the growth and joy of faith in the community.

Perhaps in this perspective we can respond to those who think that infant baptism is not easily reconciled with a consistent personalistic theology. Infant baptism can be seen as a visible sign that it is God who takes the initiative. The one God and Father, in view of the one Redeemer and brother of all men, reaches out to this child to call him through the family of believers. The community of faith, hope, and love celebrates the baptism and vows to respect this child as a son or daughter of God, to make him aware gradually, to the extent that he can understand them, of all the wondrous things that God has decreed for him or her, and to encourage this new member of God's family to respond increasingly to the good news throughout his whole life. Thus infant baptism is a solemn appeal to the community and to each member of it to "let everyone of you please his neighbor for his edification, for Christ did not please Himself" (Rom. 15:3).

We rightly emphasize that faith is a personal response in

freedom; we are not Christians because of a statistic or because our name is registered in the baptismal book. But we do not forget that, before our decision to accept the saving message, God manifests his design to bring us to the full awareness that we belong to his family, the community of faith and love.

However, if we want to be consistent in our personalistic outlook, we need to reexamine a number of problems bearing on infant baptism. I will mention only two. According to the latest Canon Law regulations on mixed marriages, a marriage between a person baptized in the Catholic Church and a person baptized in another Church or not baptized at all is still automatically invalid—that is, not recognized by the Church and without any support for its stability; it is even thought to be bereft of sacramental grace if the canonical form is not observed or dispensation is not sought and given. This holds true even for those persons who have never received any education in Catholic beliefs or the Christian faith. Thus, the baptismal register alone decides the question of validity with no respect for a personal decision or a personal faith.

Another example relates to the Canon Law definition of the conditions for a marriage to be *ratum et consummatum*— that is, sacramental and finalized, and therefore absolutely indissoluble: both persons are baptized; and the penis of the husband has penetrated the vagina of the wife. Here, too, Canon Law fails to ask whether baptism has become an event making the person aware of his belonging to the new and everlasting covenant. Much needs to be said about the criterion of *matrimonium consummatum*. Other chapters of this book may shed sufficient light on the point.

The "law of faith" means openness and solidarity. It is an encounter with God, Father of all men, and with Christ the Redeemer, who bears the burden of all mankind and who, through the grace of the Holy Spirit, gathers us all in his name. The real event of faith breaks down all barriers—artificial enclosures, grilles, castes—and opens man to his fellow men, to the world created for all by the one Father. Faith is a "light to the world" brought by people who wish not to possess the world but to enrich it by bringing Christ's love into it.

Thus, a Christian personalism affirms the uniqueness of each person whom God calls by his name to the community of faith, hope, and love. It is an appeal to those who know their name to enrich the Church and world in response to God's gifts; it is an appeal to the Church to renew constantly her structures so that they can foster a fully personal life for all. The dynamism of faith will then be reflected in a world shaped by believers.

The "law of faith" and the "law of grace" are related to each other: the same reality is seen from different angles. It is always God's gracious initiative, persons in dialogue, openness, and response-responsibility, always a Thou-I relationship with God, wherein God and his calling bring home to us the uniqueness of our name in a We-Thou-I relationship within the people of God.

18

THE LAW OF GROWTH
AND CONTINUAL
CONVERSION

THE Gospel of Jesus Christ is dynamic; it shocks those obsessed by a security complex, self-complacency, or any form of clinging to a status quo. In the past, however, a certain bourgeois mentality, marked by legalism, formalism, and an exaggerated concern for the preservation of structures and institutions, has to a great extent concealed or blocked the real dynamism of faith. Today's tremendously energetic society and the impatience of modern youth may be the "grace of the present hour" by which the dynamic aspect of Christian personalism will be rediscovered.

The genuinely Christian life of persons and communities is marked by a "law of growth" which has its dynamics in faith and grace. When God does not turn his countenance away from the sinner or the sinning community, when he reveals himself and his design in ever-new ways and ever more clearly to his friends, then joyous faith and hope respond to his graciousness by a constant process of conversion and growth.

We are led to contribute more and more generously and effectively to the development of a better, more personalized world.

Christian life celebrates hope in gratitude and thanksgiving for God's marvelous deeds, in eager expectation of fulfillment in the new earth and new heaven. In this perspective, believers experience the dynamism of the here and now, the sometimes modest, sometimes tremendous opportunities to profit by the past, to reshape its material, repair its faults, and build hope for the future.

The time of salvation in which we live is a moment of tension between the "already" and the "not yet." God has already manifested the full extent of his love in Jesus Christ and now directs our hope and our energies toward the ever-new forms of his coming and toward his final coming and the full revelation that we are his sons and daughters—and are, therefore, brothers and sisters living in a fraternal, fully personalized world.

Christian hope makes us neither dreamers nor perfectionists; it urges us to seek, in the present moment of favor, the next step in the direction clearly indicated by faith and grace. For those who have come to the full consciousness of faith, this moment of decision is a personal call from God, a chance for a personal response, a time of infinite fruitfulness, a time of grace and growth.

The theme of growth appears in several parables on the kingdom of God. The kingdom of God is like a mustard seed, the smallest of seeds, which grows into a tree large enough for birds to roost among its branches (Matt. 13:31-32). It is like yeast which a woman mixes with half a hundredweight of flour until all is leavened (Matt. 13:33). If a man hears the word, it is like seed that falls on good soil and accordingly bears fruit and yields a hundredfold or sixtyfold or thirtyfold (Matt. 13:23). The whole of Christian life is a manifestation of the dynamics of the kingdom of God. Its growth in us means that gradually God's love takes hold of us; we become leaven in the community, and each of us can yield a harvest "according to the measure of grace Christ has bestowed upon us" (Eph. 4:7).

DIFFERENCE BETWEEN STATIC AND
DYNAMIC PERSPECTIVES

Because God distributes his gifts in great variety, Christian pedagogy does not permit the imposition of the same measure on all. The prodigal son coming from afar is not expected to bear immediately the same rich harvest as those who have an excellent heritage, excellent education, who live in a harmonious family, in a good environment—although it might well happen that the tremendous experience of forgiveness may bear an extraordinary harvest of gratitude and therefore of generosity.

There has to be constant vigilance against a legalism that measures all men by the same yardstick or that calls for the immediate harvest of a total conversion—chiefly a conversion to the moralist's complicated code—before granting a poor man who comes from afar an experience of trust, hope, and love. This static morality buries four of the five talents which some have received for the benefit of all, and discourages others who would like to take the first faltering step on the way back to the Father.

In several of my writings I have warned against this "morality" which ignores the law of grace and of growth, as the ancients warned in their story of Procrustes, that mythical innkeeper of old Greek wisdom who tried to fit everyone into the same size bed. To keep everything uniform and orderly, he cut off the feet or the heads of those guests who were too tall for his beds, and stretched the limbs of the short ones, so that everything was neat—except, of course, for the blood!

The people who exhibit a Procrustean mentality are not all churchly people; the secular city is full of them. Are not the prison systems in many countries full of such types? A vindictive society knows how to measure accurately a "vindictive justice," but it makes no examination of conscience about the social causes of increasing criminality. It does not give the poor victim a chance to recover. The man who cannot pay the hundred-dollar fine goes to jail and gradually accumulates a long record in the files, while the rich one easily takes the small amount from his pocket for the same transgression of the law.

But if Christians are to be "salt for the earth," they have to begin an examination of themselves and of the attitudes and structures still existing in the Church. There is the teacher of moralism—rather than of moral theology, which he should be teaching—who presumes to know exactly the point where venial sin ends and mortal sin begins; he knows it by inches and ounces, without considering the situation or condition of persons. In rare cases he may, with condescension, acknowledge that the person has committed only an "objective" mortal sin rather than a "subjective" one, but the "objective" clothing is made according to an established pattern, without the different statures first being looked at. Priests, parents, and others in authority who follow this line are crippling those entrusted to them.

A man who prefers his own narrow measurements to the way in which God manifests his loving will by the very variety of his gifts is not a religious man. He presents God as immobile or as an eternal policeman; he does not proclaim the message of the living God, who calls everybody to a life of growth. There is no moral geometry that can apply to every human situation—to those to whom God has entrusted five or three talents as well as to those who are invited to be faithful stewards of only one talent. The genuine measure of morality lies within the self: one's gifts, one's capacities, one's experiences viewed in the presence of the giver of all good gifts and the Father of all men.

Since a moral theology according to the yardstick was at least partially due to overemphasis on the Church regulation (Council of Trent) that a person is not allowed to receive the eucharist without previous confession if he is conscious of having committed a mortal sin, a personalistic theology cannot avoid confrontation with that problem.

We must see that part of the problem lies in the transition from a closed and controlled society to a pluralistic society requiring a much greater measure of personal maturity and therefore a different approach toward moral theology. For the man come of age, the chief attention will not be given to the problems of the confessional; the criterion will be a call to maturity. But in view of the Church law and the right attitude with regard to reception of the eucharist, criteria must be offered for Christians who wish to evolve from the ethics of the yardstick to an ethics of responsibility. The question is: "Were you fully aware that this action could not be reconciled with your being a friend of God, and did you, in full awareness and with sufficient freedom, choose your selfish decision over being a friend of God?" If a person knows his own fundamental attitude, he can use this as a proximate or tentative measure of the gravity of his action. If he was still struggling before committing the fault, and almost immediately after committing it makes an act of contrition renewing his good purpose, there is enough probability that, despite his weakness, he has not turned away from God.

When the prodigal son comes from afar and is embraced by the heavenly Father, there may still be many defects in him. In some things he may already be heroic, but in others he is still without light. Many of his attitudes are outside the ideal circuit of love, but his fundamental attitude, his faith, his gratitude, locate him within the circle of salvation. His face is turned to God. By earnestly taking those first homeward steps, accompanied by an attitude of trust in "my Father," he is already in his Father's house. But we cannot propose to him, the moment he returns to sacramental life, a whole code of perfections. In the parable, the dynamic power is in the reception, the feast for the returning son, and this is expected to bring the harvest; but the harvest needs time.

The situation can be illustrated by the attitudes of a group of social workers who dedicate their lives to the rescue of prostitutes. If one of these unfortunate girls has come to the point of limiting sexual relations to one friend, the social worker will show appreciation of this enormous progress. Later, at an opportune time, she will urge the girl to think whether this friend is ready to marry, and if not, to free herself from him in view of possible marriage with another. As another example consider parents whose divorced daughter had turned to a disgraceful life of promiscuity, but later establishes a stable relationship with a good man whom she marries in a civil ceremony. They will not protest, although the Catholic Church considers her marriage canonically invalid. They will rather appreciate their daughter's great step forward.

This is, however, a very different approach from the one that seeks to breach the law, to break down all criteria by saying that adultery, promiscuity, even rape, can be sometimes good and sometimes bad. A person is not really on the way to conversion if he simply considers as good his own faults or behavior which is, in fact, far from being a genuine and full expression of true love. A dynamic pastoral approach must not be confused with the lawless situation ethics of self-complacency, when the whole situation calls for humility and for a constant striving toward higher moral standards.

Christian morality is the taking of each step as it can be taken. On earth, man will never reach the highest point; he will never be able to say, "Now I really love my neighbor as much as Christ has loved him."

But a genuine Christian always makes the next advance, always strives toward a better understanding of what faith and love demand, and measures his striving in view of the full goal. The deadly thing is to fail to strive, to remain self-satisfied, complacent, self-righteous, or to fall into despair.

THE FIRST CONVERSION AND CONTINUAL CONVERSION

The whole Christian life can be synthesized in the "law of continual conversion."

In biblical terminology, "conversion" often means that God turns his face to man and this calls and enables man to return to God with all his heart, mind, and will. Tradition distinguishes the first and basic conversion from the second or "continuing" conversion.

The first conversion has a sacramental sign in baptism. Christ calls his death a "baptism," and indeed baptism is the great "conversion" or transformation from death to life, the great sign that God's saving love is calling all men to him. This first conversion of a person in the sacrament of faith is the fundamental, initial response in faith, hope, and love. When, after baptism, a person turns to the realm of evil and has to repeat—reiterate—his first conversion, this is called a "reiterated first conversion."

What we call the "second conversion" is something different, in that it is a constant process of bringing the baptismal event into the full existential "Yes." It represents an encounter and union with God in an ongoing effort to become fully what we are called to be: sons and daughters of God, growing toward that full maturity which is "measured by nothing less than the full stature of Christ" (Eph. 4:13).

This second conversion is also called a "continual conversion," one of the most important expressions to be found in Christian tradition. Realization of the need for this lifelong effort protects men from falling into the dangerous attitude of self-righteousness, the temptation to think, "I have fulfilled this." The great commandments of the Sermon on the Mount and the Farewell Discourses are never completely fulfilled; they always have to be better fulfilled.

Continual conversion implies not simply growth; it also means purification, separation from the selfish self, conversion to our true self as meant by God, with the goal of greater union with God and greater generosity toward our neighbors.

We do not apply the word "conversion" to Christ. As Jesus grew up, he "advanced in favor with God and men" (Luke 2:40), but his progress in human experience cannot be called conversion, since he was holy from the beginning; he had no sin. Nor do we use this expression with reference to the Blessed Virgin. But for each of us and for the Church as a whole there is a constant need for struggle, renewal, reform, and conversion. It is a feature of the eschatological separation in this interim time of patience and striving, the time left to us for salvation.

In the parables on the kingdom of God (Matt. 13:1-30), a sower went out to sow. Some seeds fell by the wayside and the birds ate them, and some fell on rocky ground. Some fell among thistles. The Lord thus warns us against the danger that his message and grace may be stifled both by the environment and by our own bad soil, our selfish desires. The same warning is given in the parable of the man who sowed good seed in his field, but then an enemy came and sowed cockle. Not only in our environment but also within ourselves there is, besides all the good, much cockle. Our situation is not that we are holy and the environment is mixed; the mixture goes through the environment and through our own egos.

Our time of salvation, the time between the first and the final coming of the Lord, is called a time of separation, as in the prophecy of Simeon (summing up the whole prophetic tradition) to Mary, the mother of Christ: "Behold this child is destined for the fall and rise of many in Israel and for a sign that is contradicted" (Luke 2:34). Like Mary, those who follow him closely will discover that "a sword will pierce through your own soul also." Wherever people come in contact with Christ and his true disciples, "the secret thoughts of many hearts will be laid bare" (Luke 2:35).

Especially at the present time, which is characterized by such deep and rapid transformations and great tensions in the secular world as well as by a profound effort toward reform and renewal in the Church, we must be more fully aware of this aspect of human history. Not everything modern or "liberal" is, *ipso facto,* good, just as not everything "traditional" is good either. There should be neither pessimism nor a naïve optimism about what is going on. What we need is discernment and courage to make our choice for the right kind of renewal.

Our image of Christ must not be one-sided. He is not only the Judge, nor is he a "yes-sayer" with respect to distorted human attitudes and institutions. He is the *Prophet* who speaks truth to all, puts everything in the full light and under the saving judgment of the good news. He is the Good Shepherd but is also a "stumbling block, a stone rejected by the builders"; he is a wholesome scandal for the self-righteous.

Christian existentialism is aware of this separation and call to decision, and knows that we have constantly to make our choice, a choice not easy for the son or daughter of Adam and Eve. In Rom. 8:2 ff., Paul classically expresses this continuing call to decision when, after declaring that "the law of the life-giving Spirit has liberated us from the law of sin," he makes clear that even after this liberation we are still tempted by our selfishness; we have constantly to make a choice. "Those who live according to a self-centered nature have their outlook formed by it, and that spells death" (Rom. 8:5). (I translate the Greek word *sarx* as "self-centered nature." Some older translations have "flesh," which would confine the unworthiness to the body.) In biblical language, what is meant is a selfish way of living, an egocentric nature and outlook which is at enmity with God, refusing to subject itself to the order of love. This is the attitude that spells death. "But the spiritual outlook brings life and peace" (Rom. 8:6). This means a wholly changed perspective, a new fundamental option. And in this new attitude we are no longer subject, like slaves, to man-made law. Through the dynamism of constant growth, we fulfill the values specified and protected by laws.

In the process of continual conversion, we change gradually from egocentric personalism to selflessness. We begin "to live on the level of the Spirit," no longer content with the narrow thinking of our own self-fulfillment or concern for our own happiness. But ours will not be a joyless life. The good news of the Gospel opens us ever more to the joy which is inherent in love. We escape the frustrations of an outlook that encounters prohibitions everywhere. We live in a perspective of gratitude for all we have been given, for the fundamental free choice of self-surrender and service. And this is true joy and peace.

The law of growth and continual conversion through faith and grace leads to a vital responsiveness and responsibility. The existential personalist has no desire for a monotonous life, a static, secure routine that desires to make no response to the wonders of God's living, changing world. Especially at the present time, the true Christian desires a venturesome life that answers God's call for this time and place, employing the unique gifts which divine providence has granted to him alone. If, instead of this, we offer youth only a "holy rule" that remains forever "as it was in the beginning," having no pertinence here and now, then our appeal will be only to sick people suffering from a security complex.

INDEX